THE GUIDE TO ELECTRONIC FUTURES TRADING

THE GUIDE TO ELECTRONIC FUTURES TRADING

Scott Slutsky

Darrell Jobman

McGraw-Hill

New York   San Francisco   Washington, D.C.   Auckland   Bogotá
Caracas   Lisbon   London   Madrid   Mexico City   Milan
Montreal   New Delhi   San Juan   Singapore
Sydney   Tokyo   Toronto

McGraw-Hill

A Division of The McGraw·Hill Companies

1 2 3 4 5 6 7 8 9 0   AGM/AGM   9 0 9 8 7 6 5 4 3 2 1 0 9

ISBN 0-07-135312-7

Printed and bound by Quebecor Graphics.

McGraw-Hill books are available at special quantity discounts to use as premiums and sales promotions, or for use in corporate training programs. For more information, please write to the Director of Special Sales, McGraw-Hill, 11 West 19th Street, New York, NY 10011. Or contact your local bookstore.

This publication is designed to provide accurate and authoritative information in regard to the subject matter covered. It is sold with the understanding that neither the author not the publisher is engaged in rendering legal, accounting, or other professional service. If legal advice or other expert assistance is required, the services of a competent professional person should be sought.
—*From a Declaration of Principles jointly adopted by a Committee of the American Bar Association and a Committee of Publishers.*

This book is printed on recycled, acid-free paper containing a minimum of 50% recycled, de-inked fiber.

TRADEMARKS AND SERVICE MARKS

Company and product names associated with listings in this book should be considered as trademarks or service marks of the company indicated. The use of a registered trademark is not permitted for commercial purposes without the permission of the company named. In some cases, products of one company are offered by other companies and are presented in a number of different listings in this book. It is virtually impossible to identify every trademark or service mark for every product and every use, but we would like to highlight the following:

Exchange names, abbreviations, and in some cases, their acronyms should be considered registered trademarks of the exchanges indicated.

S&P, S&P 500, and S&P 500 Index are registered trademarks of the McGraw-Hill Companies Inc. and have been licensed for use by the Chicago Mercantile Exchange.

Nasdaq, Nasdaq 100, and Nasdaq 100 Index are trademarks of the Nasdaq Stock Market and are licensed for use by the Chicago Mercantile Exchange.

Dow Jones, The Dow, Dow Jones Industrial Average, and DJIA are service marks of Dow Jones & Company Inc. and have been licensed for use for certain purposes by the Board of Trade of the City of Chicago.

Globex, Globex$_2$, TOPS, CUBS, CUBS2, and E-mini are trademarks of the Chicago Mercantile Exchange.

Project A is a trademark of the Board of Trade of the City of Chicago.

ACCESS is a trademark of the New York Mercantile Exchange.

LIFFE CONNECT is a registered trademark of the London International Financial Futures Exchange.

Microsoft, Windows, and Windows NT are registered trademarks of Microsoft Corp.

Macintosh and Mac are registered trademarks of Apple Computer Co.

TradeStation, OptionStation, SuperCharts, ProSuite 2000i, and RadarScreen are trademarks of Omega Research Inc.

MetaStock and related names are trademarks of Equis International Inc.

DTN, DTNstant, and related names are trademarks of Data Transmission Network Corp.

Signal, eSignal, and related names are trademarks of Data Broadcasting Corp.

LeoWeb, iTrade, Market Voice, INFOLine, and Account Information Manager are trademarks of Linnco Futures Group (LFG) LLC.

Internet Order Express, Internet Order Express Millenium, Sim-U-Trade, and VACIS are trademarks of Vision LP.

RJOCAT is a trademark of R. J. O'Brien & Associates Inc.

BEST Direct, DayTRADER Pro, and TurnKey IB are trademarks of Peregrine Financial Group.

Auditrade is a trademark of Auditrack Inc.

GTEX is a trademark of DH Financial LLC.

Theodore is a registered trademark of Linleigh Group Ltd. and is used with permission by Rand Financial Services Inc.

ifutures and Swarm Technology are registered trademarks of Professional Services Division of Rosenthal Collins Group LLC.

This book is dedicated to all the floor traders, clerks, runners, and other trading floor personnel—including many from multigenerational trading families—who helped to build the futures industry into what it is today and now face some difficult adjustments in a new era of trading.

CONTENTS

PREFACE   xi
ACKNOWLEDGMENTS   xiii
FOREWORD   xv
INTRODUCTION   xvii

Chapter 1

What the Electronic Trader Needs   1

Chapter 2

Making Your Decision—Pretrade Analysis   7
Hardware   8
Computers   8
Distribution Systems   9
Data and Information   13
Trading Platforms   16
Futures 'Portals'   21
Price Quotes   24
Real-Time Data   26
End-of-Day, Historical Data   31
News, Publications, and Other Interesting Sources   33
Publications   34
Other Information Sources   39
Organizations, Regulators, Government   43
Forums, Chats, Newsgroups   46
Analytical Software   48
A Word About Trading Systems   49
Analytical Software   52

Chapter 3

Handling Your Order—The Brokerage Connection   71
Online Screens   78
Key Questions   83
Final Evaluation   85
Online Futures Brokerage Firms   89

Chapter 4

Executing Your Trade—The Exchange Function   133

Background   133
Chicago Mercantile Exchange   142
Chicago Board of Trade   144
New York Mercantile Exchange   148
Cantor Exchange   148
Eurex   148
London International Financial Futures and
Options Exchange (LIFFE)   149
Sydney Futures Exchange   151

Chapter 5

Defining Your Style—Methods for Electronic Trading   155

Stops and Other Orders   156
Electronic Trading Approaches   161

Chapter 6

Trading Rules for Electronic Traders   177

Chapter 7

The Last Chapter... or the Next Chapter?   185

ABOUT THE AUTHORS   193
INDEX   195

For any futures trader who has ever wished he or she didn't have to talk with a broker or deal with floor traders, electronic trading may sound like a dream. For some who have tried it, however, it may seem more like a nightmare, not so much because of the pressures of trading but the stress of technology.

The purpose of this book is to bring trading and technology together to show you what electronic trading is today and what it can be in the future. This is not a book for traders looking for a computer geek help to pick the right computer with the right amount of RAM running at the right megahertz with the right DVD drives or USB buses or other peripherals. Beyond a few basic items covered here, computer magazines or online catalogs are better resources for hardware-related matters.

This also is not the book for the technology whiz to learn how to trade just because he or she has a computer and wants to jump into one of the hottest investment areas today. Strategies for online trading are covered in a growing number of books, advisory services, and seminars. We touch on how some methods apply to electronic trading, but you will need to refer to other sources to assess which of those might be most helpful, just as you would when approaching any new endeavor.

Instead, this book is for traders who use or want to use their computers to facilitate and improve their futures trading. It focuses on all the things you need to consider to become an electronic trader and presents a number of choices for setting up your online trading operation.

Several other points need to be emphasized up front:

- This book only covers futures trading. It does not get into day trading the hottest Internet stocks or other equities, but it could attract speculators from that arena to stock index futures as another fast-paced alternative.
- Anything electronic involving the Internet can change very quickly, and that is true of the information in this book. New technology, new Web sites, new alignments in the futures industry, and many other factors will make change a constant part of trading over the next few years. We have tried to make this book as accurate and as current as possible, but what you see here will need to be updated continuously.

- Although the book lists a number of companies and services, we do not attempt to rate them or recommend one over another. Virtually everything will fit someone, so you will need to make your own evaluation to see what fits you best.

With that background, we hope this book will help you prepare for an exciting venture into electronic trading, the future of futures trading!

Scott Slutsky
Darrell Jobman

ACKNOWLEDGMENTS

With a topic as broad and as pervasive in the futures industry today as electronic trading, it is difficult to pinpoint the origin of all the ideas, opinions, and information that were useful in putting together what you will see in the following pages. This book would not have been possible without the resources provided on the Internet, of course, so the first expression of thanks goes to all those who create and especially maintain the thousands of Internet pages related to trading and to those responsible for seeing that the information gets online.

We interviewed many people and received support and ideas from others not listed here. At the risk of overlooking someone, we would particularly like to acknowledge the contributions of the following people and in some cases, their staffs:

Brokerage Firms   Barry Lind and Barbara Richards, Lind-Waldock & Co.; Bill Kaiser, ZAP Futures; Ira Epstein, Ira Epstein & Co. Futures; Jerome Bressert, BEST Direct Division of Peregrine Financial Group; Bill Massey, LFG LLC; Glen Swanson, Futures Online; Joe Tapias, Trade Center; Mike Greenberg, Alaron Trading Corp.; Chuck Bohm, First American Discount Corp.; Lori O'Connor, Interactive Brokers; Tom Zabroske, DH Financial LLC; Jeff Quinto, Rand Financial Services; Donna Kline, Fox Investments; Bert Meyer, Jack Carl Futures; Marty Badiola, PMB Inc.; Paul Moran, Rosenthal Collins Group.

Exchanges   Arthur Tursh and Kevin Donegan, Chicago Mercantile Exchange; Andrew Zagorski, Chicago Board of Trade.

Traders   Chuck Reeder, Larry Rosenberg, Larry Mollner, Greg Antonucci, Jeffrey Biegel, Jeremy Perlow, and a trading coach, Adrienne Laris Toghraie, president of Trading on Target and author of several books on the psychology of trading.

Data, Software   Amy Solt, Omega Research Inc.; Sheennan Showers, Data Broadcast Corp./eSignal.

And we would like to say a special thanks to Jack Sandner, president of RB&H Financial Services and special policy advisor and former chairman of the Chicago Mercantile Exchange, for writing the foreword, and to Marrietta Sorensen of the RB&H staff for her assistance.

The miraculous marriage of technology and consumers is creating a world with boundless opportunity. It's a digital universe where geography, time, and space are irrelevant; where information and analysis are ubiquitous and in real-time; where invention, discovery, and obsolescence are an everyday event; where market expansion is outrunning the global giants of commerce.

The pace of change will continue to move faster and faster. Palm Pilots, digital cellular phones, seaworthy fiber-optic cables, and microwave communications are rushing to the market. Optical and wireless bandwidth is growing at least twice as fast as Moore's Law, which doubles silicon efficiency every 18 months.

Technology has allowed ideas, information, and money to move from place to place with an ease that renders time zones and political borders seamless. The collapse of the Berlin Wall and the implosion of the Soviet bloc paved the way for the triumph of global capitalism. A new economy has been born, creating opportunity on a scale not witnessed since the industrial revolution.

Virtually overnight, some 3.5 billion new consumers and producers have been spawned. Daily, the number of economically and technologically literate individuals grows, all of them eager to exercise their skills and improve their lot in the free market. And the drumbeat for direct online access to the marketplace grows louder and louder.

The democratization of the world's marketplace is proceeding apace amid the new economy; the world has wrapped its strong and sinewy arms around free-market capitalism and it is unstoppable. The market for all goods and services is growing exponentially. The immense appetite for bonds, stocks, indexes, futures, and options is insatiable. Indeed, Arthur Levitt, the chairman of the Securities and Exchange Commission, has declared, "If futures and options didn't exist, we'd have to invent them." Electronic market makers flourish and are proliferating; discount houses, such as Schwab, E*Trade, and AmeriTrade, grow and grow; full-service securities firms are rushing to market with discount online trading services as well. We hear the daily mantra that the Internet provides individuals with instant information, instant transmission of data, and instant execution.

We are blessed to live in a time where the change that is occurring is perhaps the most important in history. But this bless-

ing can also be a curse: The extraordinary proliferation of resources and venues offering information, analyses, and execution is overwhelming.

In this rush to market, no one has thought to coherently
organize the frenzy, confusion, and abundance of the financial
marketplace. Until now! Scott Slutsky and Darrell Jobman have
authored this invaluable resource for futures traders, and it is
long overdue. They organize this proliferation of resources into a
guide for the individual who enters cyberspace to trade. This book
takes us through the electronic world, starting at the very beginning. It is a "must" reference for anyone who wants to join the
growing number of entrepreneurs, risk managers, and asset
allocators in the futures trading arena. The authors describe how
to start and where to get information, analytical software, and
trading systems. They provide links to Internet sites of vendors
that can help with pretrade analysis and of brokerage services
for electronic trading. They examine exchanges that offer electronic trading systems, order routing, and order matching.

This book is a must for aspiring electronic futures traders,
especially as we go into the millennium. It is as important to the
trader as a dictionary is to a student, a thesaurus is to a writer,
or a Bible is to a preacher. This book will save the trader count-
less hours. Scott Slutsky and Darrell Jobman sort out the services offered, simplify their complexity, and identify the
competitive spin. Most important, they help the trader avoid costly
mistakes.

> *Jack Sandner*
> *President, RB&H Financial Services*
> *Former Chairman and now*
> *Special Policy Advisor of the*
> *Chicago Mercantile Exchange*

Imagine you are a futures trader in an ideal world . . . in a galaxy far, far away . . .

> . . . your computer hasn't told you in months that you have performed an "illegal operation."
>
> . . . your connections to your telephone, electricity, cable TV, satellite dish, or Internet service provider have all been performing flawlessly.
>
> . . . you have all the accurate data and information you need to make a trading decision.
>
> . . . your Holy Grail trading system was easy to develop, with simple, clear instructions from the software program's manual.
>
> . . . your system tells you to go long at the exact bottom of the market.
>
> . . . one click of your mouse and your trade is executed at the precise price you wanted—no slippage and low commission charges.
>
> . . . another click and you know exactly what your filled position is moments after the order is executed.
>
> . . . your Holy Grail trading system flashes a sell signal to get you out of your long position at the top tick of the market.
>
> . . . again, one click to send your sell order and in an instant, your fill shows up on your screen. You are out of the market with a big profit.

Has that ever happened to anyone? The Holy Grail trading system portion of the scenario is quite plausible, of course (tongue in cheek here). Such systems would seem to be abundant, judging by the direct mail packages and magazine and television advertisements that traders see and hear every day. What is almost more improbable than the elusive perfect trading system is that technology would allow the trade decision and execution process to take place so quickly and efficiently.

For any futures trader, the stress of trading itself usually is enough of a challenge, especially in volatile markets when prices and conditions are changing rapidly. But for the electronic trader, trading stress may actually take a back seat to what has been termed "technostress," the kind of stress that ties up your insides when your computer freezes up or your broker's order-entry system goes down just when your position is losing ground the fastest. It's the emotion you have to endure when trying to cope with technology that is still trying to advance enough to make futures trading online go easily and smoothly consistently.

The key word is "consistently." The biggest benefit of trading electronically is the speed and efficiency you get when everything works. The biggest frustration is when it doesn't, a situation that is still too common today for both futures traders and officials in the futures industry to be totally comfortable trading electronically.

This is not to paint a discouraging picture of electronic trading, because there are examples of how well it can work, and it truly is the wave of the future. However, any futures trader who wants to take advantage of all the things electronic trading will eventually offer must deal with the realities of where it is today. And, frankly, the status of electronic trading in the futures industry today is about where traveling by automobile across the United States was in the 1920s or going cross-country by air was in the 1930s.

When Bill Kaiser, president of ZAP Futures in Chicago, started in the futures industry in 1968 as a runner at the Chicago Mercantile Exchange, prices were posted on chalkboards, and Polaroid camera photos were used for official time and sales reports. That was about the time, he recalls, that Pong, the first big computer video game, was introduced, followed by Pac-Man a few years later. In the 30-plus years since then, you know the unimaginable levels to which Nintendo, Sega, Sony, and others have taken video games, but electronic trading in the futures industry is still in the Pac-Man stage, to use Kaiser's description.

When you turn on an electric switch, you don't have to know anything about substations or fuses or anything else to light up a room. When you use the telephone, you don't have to know about access codes, modem configurations, preferences, or anything else other than that you have to punch a few numbers to talk to another party. When you turn on a television, you don't have to know about pixels, installation instructions, drives, or anything else to view a program you want.

Of course, those technologies have taken years to develop to today's level. Electronic trading is still relatively new and based on a very fragile thread, often depending on communication links and technological expertise that are not yet suited to the pressures of active trading. The good news is that electronic trading is making rapid strides on the equities side, even with the occasional widely publicized brokerage firm outages on heavy trading days. The number of online accounts was estimated at about 7 million in the first quarter of 1999, and online brokerages executed about a half million trades per day during that quarter, according to research by U.S. Bancorp Piper Jaffray analyst Stephen Franco. So something right must be happening.

The rapid growth of online trading in equities is moving into futures and will overcome the industry's technological and political obstacles because the primary force driving the futures industry to electronic trading is the same thing that is pushing online trading in equities—basic economics.

From the exchange perspective, the open-outcry trading system has served well for many years. However, everything about the system becomes strained when exchanges have to increase volume to maintain profits and remain competitive in world markets. There are only so many bodies that can be crowded into so little space with only so much time available. By necessity, today's exchanges and their physical facilities have to become more efficient at handling more trading if they want to stay in business. The survival instinct is reason enough for exchanges to be interested in electronic trading.

From the brokerage firm perspective, competition to attract trading customers is intense, and one of the main lures is low commission rates. In the push to lower rates, brokerage firms have to use anything they can to improve their efficiency, so handling orders electronically with fewer people is naturally appealing if they want to remain in the picture. Economy of scale issues already have affected the brokerage industry as firms merge or find other services to offer their customers.

From the individual trader perspective, electronic trading may be an answer to frustrations traders have endured with brokers and floor traders for many years. Right or wrong, traders have long perceived that some of those people on the phones and in the pits were out to get a chunk of their money, running their stops and churning their accounts. Unfortunately, if you wanted to trade, there was only one game in town for most markets, resulting in a my-way-or-no-way attitude that sometimes embittered traders to the futures industry. So if electronic trading can cut out any of those middle people, it naturally is appealing to individual traders.

How will all of these interests mesh together in an electronic trading world? Do electronic traders even need exchanges for their trading? Do they need brokerage firms to handle their trades? Those are longer-term issues we'll cover in later chapters.

Dealing with today first, this appears to be an ideal time to prepare for electronic futures trading, for a number of reasons:

- More U.S. contracts will be traded electronically as existing exchanges and many new electronic communications networks expand their trading hours. Internationally, electronic trading has virtually become the norm. Screen trading doesn't have the same dynamics as pit trading, and as electronic trading takes over a growing share of the U.S. market, you will need to train yourself to be on the leading edge.

- More brokerage firms are geared up for online trading, and active traders will need to be familiar with online order-entry procedures.

- Stock index futures could become very attractive to investors when—not if—the stock market turns bearish or stagnates. We don't need to go into all the advantages of including futures in an investment account, but the fact that you can go short as easily as long in futures and with much less margin money than in stocks should appeal to those who are holding or trading stocks when the appeal of the stock market fades.

- The Internet has become the key mechanism for distributing data and information. This reservoir of information is growing daily, just waiting to be tapped by traders. Someday it may even include free price quotes as futures exchanges, like stock exchanges, discover that low (or no) fees for quotes could attract more traders and more volume.

- Faster Internet access is coming to many more communities, making new and improved services available to electronic traders. The only question is who will get there first, the telephone companies, the cable TV carriers, or some other technological innovation that will advance the communications revolution.

Welcome to electronic trading. Welcome to futures. Welcome to the future.

CHAPTER 1

What the Electronic Trader Needs

Nearly every form of investing is based on three essential components:

- Money
- Mentality
- Method

Money is a rather obvious requirement for any investment and may dictate the direction of the other two elements.

Mentality deals with personality and the ability to handle various investment approaches.

Method involves all the pieces needed to put your money and your mentality to work in a market environment.

We cannot do a lot about the amount of money or the mindset you bring to the table, but this book can help you prepare for a method that focuses on a trading philosophy in a market that offers huge opportunities.

If you are a stamp collector, you may be interested in rare stamps, but the funds you have will likely be important in determining whether those are the kinds of stamps you can buy. If you do have the funds and get a rare stamp, the satisfaction you get from just having it in your safe and pulling it out to look at it once in a while may be all you want. Or your satisfaction may come from the amount of money you can make by passing it along to someone else willing to pay you more than you paid for the stamp.

The same concept holds true in real estate or stocks or many other investments: Are you buying for income (rent, dividends, etc.) or for long-term appreciation or just for the possibility of converting a quick buck? Some people can deal with one form of investment but not another. Psychologically, they just may not have the personal characteristics it takes to be suited for a more active trading style of investment.

Not everyone can be a short-term, electronic trader in the futures markets. First and foremost, you must have a trading mentality and not a buy-and-hold philosophy. That means you never fall in love with any position or investment, and you are willing to accept losses as part of a successfully implemented trading strategy.

Chuck Reeder, an independent trader in a North Shore community near Chicago, formerly traded in the pits at a futures exchange. As trading in futures quieted down, he found that his particular style of trading was better suited to trading individual stocks that became much more volatile in the 1990s. As a trader, Reeder needed something that moved.

"Stocks [in 1999] are where commodities were in the 1970s," he said in explaining his choice of trading instruments.

When stock market conditions change, then futures may again be a more attractive trading vehicle to him, and he can move back into that arena. The key is that he has the psychological makeup of a trader and is more comfortable with that approach to the markets. You may have to do the same type of self-analysis and may even want to read about the psychological aspects of trading in other books.

Even if you conclude you have the characteristics necessary to be a trader, you have to sort out whether you are more comfortable as a position trader or as a short-term in-and-out trader in a market that can be mind numbingly dull one minute and so fast-paced the next that it will make your head spin. The difference for the electronic trader often is time: As a trader, you exist either among the quick or the dead.

Contrary to the image sometimes portrayed in the media, however, you do not have to be a "gunslinger" to be an electronic trader. You do not have to be one of those young "new investors," who use their credit cards for their stake to day trade Internet stocks. You might, in fact, be quite a normal person who believes there is more risk in holding a position overnight or longer than there is in trading in and out of a market.

The amount of money you put into your trading account depends on the type of trading you want to do, but it should be money you can afford to lose without affecting your lifestyle. A few brokerage firms will let you open an account with several thousand dollars, and many have $5000 as a minimum. But because $5000 is close to the initial margin required to trade the E-mini S&P 500 Index contract, it is not realistic to expect to trade the popular E-mini with a $5000 account. In fact, less than $20,000 or $25,000 may put too much pressure on the E-mini trader too early, according to the traders we interviewed.

Only you can determine whether you have the money and the mindset to be an electronic trader. Assuming you are still interested in being an electronic trader, the next set of decisions you have to make involves your method of trading or the way your mind says you should put your money into play in the marketplace. Again, you will need to make choices that match your comfort level. It is absolutely essential in electronic trading that you have complete confidence in the setup you are using, because you often have to make very quick decisions.

The words "electronic trading" can mean different things to different people:

1. You have a computer and use it to receive price quotes (real-time, delayed, or end-of-day), research reports, and other market information and to analyze charts, but you still use the telephone to place orders through a broker.

2. You do everything in No. 1, but instead of calling a broker, you place your orders online without any personal contact with a broker. Your order goes to a brokerage firm order desk for screening and then is passed on to a floor trader. Your online order-entry program essentially just replaces the telephone.

3. Same as No. 2, but instead of going to an order desk where it may be reviewed and reentered before it is relayed to the floor, your order goes straight to terminals on the trading floor where it is still traded in an open-outcry forum.

4. You use your computer for real-time quotes, analysis, online order entry, etc., and orders are executed in an electronic trade-matching system, with no personal contact with a broker, no clerks, no floor traders, and no open-outcry trading floor—an end-to-end electronic transaction. This is ultimately the goal of the electronic trader, but it is available in only a few futures markets at this point.

So what does it take to become this ultimate electronic futures trader? We have divided the essential components that go into executing a trade into three broad categories in this book, organized according to their roles in the typical trading process (see Figure 1–1):

- Pretrade analysis—the components an electronic trader needs to help him or her come to a trading decision. This is the area over which the individual trader has the most control and where the Internet has been most useful.
- Placing the order—the brokerage intermediary between the trader and the trade, which is where some of the biggest advances in electronic trading occurred in 1999.
- Executing the order—the order-matching mechanism, the exchange's role in the trading process, which is where the biggest battles are still likely to take place as the move to electronic trading continues.

This list does not take into account one other critical component—you, the individual trader. We have put an electronic slant on some trading methods and rules that have served futures traders well for many years, but you will have to determine which ones fit your trading style.

FIGURE 1–1

The Trading Process

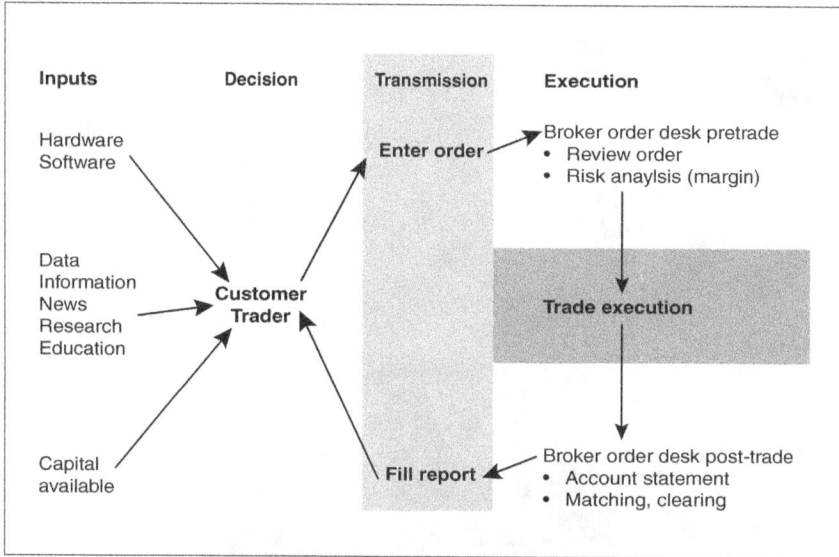

| Inputs | Decision | Transmission | Execution |

Inputs:
- Hardware
- Software
- Data
- Information
- News
- Research
- Education
- Capital available

Decision: Customer Trader

Transmission: Enter order / Fill report

Execution:
- Broker order desk pretrade
  - Review order
  - Risk anaylsis (margin)
- Trade execution
- Broker order desk post-trade
  - Account statement
  - Matching, clearing

The electronic futures trading process is like any trading process: Bring all your pretrade analyses together to make a trading decision, enter your order through a broker, have your trade executed at an exchange, and get your fill reported from your broker. The difference is that everything occurs at a much faster pace. At least, that is what electronic traders are counting on.

CHAPTER 2

Making Your Decision—
Pretrade Analysis

Any trader of any time frame needs some basis for making a trading decision, whether it's the hot tip du jour from a brother-in-law or a meticulous analysis of fundamentals.

For electronic traders, that usually means technical analysis; that is, a study of price action. That study usually leads to charts, which track prices and illustrate visually the psychology of the trading crowd as buying and selling pressure grows and diminishes in the marketplace. For short-term traders trying to position themselves to capitalize on these price changes, time is a key factor, of course, so every element of their trading program must take time into account. Getting information from the morning newspaper, a weekly newsletter, or even a daily hotline advisory service alone will not suffice. The active trader needs more than one source of information.

This section focuses on pretrade analysis—what the electronic trader needs to make a trade decision. The process is not unlike that for any type of trading. However, we focus on items that apply mostly to short-term electronic trading. Consequently, some very good products or services may not be included in our listings. The structure you put into place will depend on your style of analysis and trading and, of course, your pocketbook. These decisions are not unique to the electronic trader.

Some products and services listed on the following pages are stand-alone products; others are integrated into packages for which the tradeoff for all-in-one convenience may be higher price. For the technologically challenged, that is probably a good tradeoff. In some cases, everything the electronic trader needs may be available from a broker. Other traders may prefer to put the pieces together themselves to tailor a setup for their specific requirements.

Obviously, new services come about daily and firms change or merge, so this list can never be complete. Fortunately, the Internet has become a great shopping venue that can update you with the latest offerings and pricing.

The listing of a firm or product or service in this section should not be regarded as an endorsement or recommendation by the authors. Likewise, the fact that a firm or product or service is not included in this section should not be taken to suggest anything negative. We just may not have heard about that source at the time the book was written, or we may have concluded that the source fell outside the scope of this book. Finally, we believe all information is correct and up-to-date, but in the fast-paced world of technology and trading, we cannot guarantee that everything is current and accurate.

We probably don't need to state the obvious, but the key elements for pretrade analysis in electronic trading include:

- Hardware: a computer and some physical connection to receive and send information.
- Sources of data and information to put into your computer.
- Software that analyzes all the inputs and helps you make a trading decision.

HARDWARE

COMPUTERS

The market has pretty well dictated what kind of computer the electronic trader will have to use. Apple/Macintosh may have the better operating system, may be more stable, may be easier to use, and may be making a comeback, but because of the range of software available, electronic traders have little choice but to accept reality and go with the marketing clout of the PC/Windows combination. In fact, many software programs that would interest electronic traders are only available for the PC/Windows operating system.

In the past, many news and data vendors required you to have a dedicated terminal if you wanted to get their information, but most companies have now moved to the Internet or have made their services available on PCs. If you want to be an active trader and you want to collect and analyze thousands of bits of data for a number of markets, you want as much computer power and as much speed as you can afford. How much that is depends a great deal on what type of analysis you want to do and what programs you use for your analysis.

Vendors will often indicate lower minimums, but as a general rule of thumb for some of today's most popular programs, you should be looking at a minimum of 128 MB RAM and 300 MHz speed, with a hard drive that has at least 6 gigabytes of memory. Depending on the program, you may want to go to an NT environment.

In spite of the promises of multitasking and programs working in the background, you would be well-advised to have one computer (maybe even two) dedicated just to your trading activities and to keep your games or family programs on a separate PC. If you like to travel and trade, you might want to check into today's high-powered portable notebook computers. Some active traders use their portable as their only computer, taking it with them wherever they go and plugging in a port replicator or a mouse for easier use when they are in their office or home.

Although the hardware is an essential component of electronic trading, it should not be the basis for deciding what you will use for trading. Determine the type of trading you want to do first, then decide what software programs will help you trade before you select the computer that can handle the software.

We have no magic secrets or tips about where you get your PC. Name a supplier and you will find people who can relate good experiences and other people who can cite bad stories about their products, services, or technical support. You can go with a brand you know, or you can use one of the best shopping tools available, the Internet, which has dozens of hardware sites from the biggest, best-known names to the discount suppliers. These resources are probably more informative than anything we could present in a book.

DISTRIBUTION SYSTEMS

To borrow a phrase from real estate, the most important consideration for establishing an electronic link to the trading world may come down to "location, location, location." Some services that sound very appealing because of their speed or reliability may not be available to you yet because of where you live. In addition, the data/software source you choose may dictate the type of receiver you will need to use.

Keep in mind that no matter how fast and how powerful and how expensive a computer you buy, some tasks cannot be performed any faster than the weakest link in your communication chain. Currently, that may be the 56K modem, especially when it comes to graphics.

What is important is that you have some reliable means of getting the information you want in a timely manner. If it is important to your account that you not have any interruptions in information flow into or out of your trading site, you may want to use several of these alternatives. At this stage of technology, redundancy is a key word for futures traders, and nowhere is that more important than for an electronic trader's communication links.

"Speed" and "bandwidth" are two of today's buzzwords, especially as data sources become more extensive and sophisticated. As with computer power, it seems there can never be enough of either. The primary battle for the data delivery business is between telephone and cable services, both of which already have access to millions of homes and offices and are expanding their high-speed access services, albeit at a much slower pace than many eager Internet users would like. It should be interesting to see who will win the race to capture Internet customers.

Here is a brief description of the various data transport methods, but keep in mind the importance of geography and the fact you will have to do your own research to see what is available in your area.

Dedicated Line (Telephone)

This has been and still is the most common link to the trading world. In the past, of course, that meant POTS—plain old telephone service. Your brokers called you or you called them to deliver information or place orders.

For the electronic trader today, a dedicated line is more likely to mean a standard telephone connection to an Internet service provider (ISP), many of whom provide unlimited connect time for a fee of about $20 per month. If you travel, you may want to choose one of the national ISPs that has local phone numbers all over the country.

Aside from finding a reliable ISP that can handle your business, there are several other suggestions regarding telephone service. If you have a choice, get more than the two lines typical in most houses, especially if you trade from a home office or you have a family that also would like to use the telephone occasionally. Having four lines is probably the minimum in today's technological world. Like computer power, it doesn't seem like you can ever have too much when it comes to telephone lines (until it comes to the "wiring" and other charges telephone companies tack onto your bill for every line).

POTS doesn't provide a lot of bandwidth, but a typical analog modem today can transmit at 56.6 Kbps, fast compared to the baud rates of a few years ago, but intolerably slow if you need to download large files. If you are a power Internet user, you should definitely consider one of the faster telephone services.

ISDN and ADSL

You may not be ready for a T1 line of your own, but it is now practical for individual traders to have Integrated Services Digital Network (ISDN) or Asymmetrical Digital Subscriber Line (ADSL, but frequently referred to as DSL) service. Unfortunately, these services are not available in many areas yet, and there is a price to pay, from roughly $50 to $200 per month, depending on the bandwidth you select, plus additional charges for installation and equipment. And if you have ever dealt with the telephone company, you understand that time does not seem to be its priority. However, faster access services are expanding and prices should come down.

Telephone companies developed ADSL to compete with cable TV by delivering both TV and phone service on your plain old copper phone line. Both ADSL and cable were designed for one-way delivery of information, so their download speed is much faster than their upload speed.

DSL downloads up to 6 Mbps over the standard copper telephone lines already in most homes. Depending on the amount you are willing to pay for various levels of service, DSL's speed is comparable to ISDN and cable, and you can use the same phone line for a conversation while transmitting data. Like cable, DSL gives you a connection with the Internet 24 hours a day—no dialups. However, if you are more than about three miles from a telephone network hub, DSL service may not be available to you. Check your telephone company to see if your location has access to either ISDN or DSL service.

Cable

Another type of dedicated line is the standard coaxial cable that cable companies have spread into millions of homes to deliver television programming. With the capacity to download at 10–20 Mbps, cable has the speed advantages mentioned above already built-in, and it is available 24 hours a day with no dialing in and no extra phone line required. Some communities have built fiber-optic cable networks that offer even faster delivery.

Unfortunately, the availability of this fast alternative for Internet service is also limited, because most cable operators still need to upgrade their systems and have been slow to do so. If you are in an area where the cable TV company does provide Internet service, some active Internet users claim this is the route to go. Naturally, that depends on the reliability of the cable TV company's service, which can be erratic in some places, and the more users that get on the cable, the slower your delivery will become.

Although more data vendors are moving to Internet delivery, some do use cable TV to distribute their data, using a special box that converts cable signals into price quotes and news on your computer screen. You need to subscribe to the cable service, of course, but the cable fee is relatively low for a continuous feed of data around the clock.

Satellite Dish

The choices above may not be options for someone in a rural area, and some data/information services are delivered only via satellite. When storms or construction crews knock out phone or cable lines or the lines are burdened with heavy traffic, satellite customers do not have to worry about such things. Of course, satellites occasionally have their problems, too, and you do have to install and maintain a physical dish at your site.

Location also may be a limiting factor in that apartment or condominium buildings may not allow satellite dishes, or you may not have the southern exposure that most services require to receive the satellite signal in the United States. In general, however, satellites are an effective alternative for the electronic trader who wants to be connected to a specific data source.

Fixed Wireless or FM Signals

Like some of the other services above, location may be the most limiting factor because there needs to be a direct line of sight between the transmitting tower and the receiving customer for these types of services. Weather conditions can also affect delivery.

On the positive side, however, these setups may be easier and cheaper to install than any kind of cable or wire, and they can transmit vast amounts of data very fast. Fixed wireless can transmit up to 100 times faster than cable or DSL and up to 700 times faster than regular telephone lines, according to one press report. The point-to-multipoint technology bypasses local cable and phone systems and may become a viable alternative if it is available in a larger urban area.

DATA AND INFORMATION

For some electronic traders, prices may be all they need to make a trading decision. Every possible factor is incorporated into the current price, they reason, and all they need to know is that price to judge whether it is "high" or "low." Others will require support for their conclusions in the form of software that can produce price charts, or they may need trading systems that analyze those prices to provide trading signals. Others may need reinforcement from fundamental information provided by news reports and background research. Still others will rely primarily on the commentary and recommendations of brokers or advisory services.

Typically, active traders need to have access to three basic elements:

1. **Price quotes.** The foundation of any serious trading program is fast, accurate, reliable price quotes. If you do not have complete confidence in your price quotes, it is very difficult to set up a successful trading plan, especially for electronic trading. As you make decisions about a broker, analytical software, or other aspects of your trading program, where you will get your price quotes should be a central consideration in your search process. In fact, it probably should be your No. 1 concern. You cannot afford gaps in your data; you need to know where the market is. If your data is faulty, your charts will be faulty, your trading system signals will be faulty, and all your analysis will be based on faulty premises.

2. **Analysis tools.** This may mean charts that track price history, software that optimizes results from past price action or forecasts future price action, or information sources that interpret market action and put it into perspective. You need to know where the market has been and the ability to calculate where it might go.

3. **Order-entry mechanism.** You need a way to enter and exit positions and, most important, to get fill reports. You need to know where you are relative to current prices and market history.

At the current time, a brokerage firm is the only way to accomplish No. 3. As a key link between the trader and the trade, a broker also may be the only source you need for price quotes and information to conduct all of your pretrade analysis. If a firm is primarily involved in the brokerage business and delivers quotes, news, analysis, trade recommendations, etc., as part of its service, we have included its listing in the chapter on brokerages (see Chapter 3).

This section is reserved for the many other sources that could fit into the decision-making plan for any type of trader. With the growth of the Internet, the list of possibilities is endless, so we have focused on some of those that might be most useful to a short-term electronic trader. Listings are alphabetical, for the most part.

We will start with some of the more complete services that include all data and analysis tools together in one package, what can be called the trading platform types of programs that offer everything needed for your pretrade analysis. In some cases, that service comes with a hefty subscription fee for real-time data. In other cases, much of what you need may be available on one of the Internet sites that offer a variety of links and free services to the electronic trader, including some sites that are attempting to be "portals" to the futures industry.

Then we'll look at suppliers of price quotes and other data, concentrating on real-time sources. Finally, we'll cover some of the publications and other Internet resources that may be of interest to electronic traders. Many other subjects could have been covered in more detail, such as advisory services, weather services, risk analysis tools, portfolio or money management software, educational and training sources, and the like. However, the lists on the following pages should help potential electronic traders with most of their greatest concerns about getting the main components of their trading program in place.

If price history is important for your testing and analysis purposes, one important question to ask any data vendor is the amount of history that comes with its program. Daily history with some of the leading real-time quote services ranges from 1 to 15 years, and intraday history from current day only to as long as 12 months. Current day only may not be sufficient to test your short-term strategies. How long a period of history you need depends on what you want to do with it, of course, but it is a factor to keep in mind when you are pricing different data sources.

One thing you will not escape, no matter what service you choose for live, real-time quotes, is exchange fees. Stock exchanges charge a rather minimal amount, but most futures exchanges continue to charge higher fees for their quotes, considering them to be a significant revenue source for the exchange. The Chicago Mercantile Exchange became the first futures exchange to follow the stock exchanges' lead by reducing its monthly real-time fee to $10 starting in 2000, and other futures exchanges may follow. Until that happens, the total cost of real-time quotes can reach a rather hefty amount for an electronic trader (see Table 2–1).

Nevertheless, if you are an active electronic trader, you will want real-time quotes. Rather than receiving live quotes for all exchanges, however, you might consider real-time delayed quotes

TABLE 2–1

Monthly Exchange Fees

U.S. Stock Exchanges	
American Stock Exchange	$3.25
New York Stock Exchange	$5.25
Nasdaq Level I	$4.00
U.S. Futures Exchanges	
Chicago Board of Trade	$30.00
Chicago Mercantile Exchange	$10.00
Kansas City Board of Trade	$12.00
MidAmerica Commodity Exchange	$10.00
Minneapolis Grain Exchange	$13.00
New York Board of Trade	$88.00
New York Mercantile Exchange	$55.00
Commodities Exchange (division of NYMEX)	$55.00
Selected Non-U.S. Exchanges	
Eurex	$18.00
London International Financial Futures Exchange (LIFFE)— financial products	$21.00
LIFFE—commodity products	$60.00
Marche a Terme International de France	$15.00
Sydney Futures Exchange	$65.00
Singapore International Monetary Exchange	$18.00
Tokyo International Financial Futures Exchange	$25.00
Tokyo Stock Exchange	$80.00
Winnipeg Commodity Exchange	$14.00

Rate for one system. Stock exchange rates are for a "nonprofessional," that is, a person who uses the information for personal investing and does not furnish it to others in any business activity.

Source: CQG

for some exchanges (10-minute delay for Chicago exchanges, 30 minutes for New York futures exchanges), if that alternative is available. So if you wanted real-time quotes from just the two large Chicago exchanges and could get by with delayed quotes from the other exchanges, for example, you would pay a monthly fee of $40 plus the quote vendor's monthly charge.

TRADING PLATFORMS

When vendors combine price quotes, analytical software, and a number of other features together into one comprehensive package, you can expect to pay a little for the convenience. Whatever arrangement you make, real-time price quotes for futures are likely to cost you an ongoing fee for the foreseeable future as they come into your terminal. As for the analytical software to apply to the data, you can either purchase a program and own it outright or you can lease it for a monthly service fee. In other words, you never own the program but you subscribe to the right to use it.

These complete trading platform services, previously available only on the company's dedicated terminals, are generally available on personal computers today and often via the Internet. Although they typically are perceived to be a little more expensive, they also are seen as providing higher-quality service. Considering the price tag for some analytical software and allocating the cost over the months you expect to use it, the trading platform types of services may not be out of line when electronic traders look at their monthly expenses. One bonus of the trading platform is you only have to deal with one vendor—the data service can't claim it's a software problem or the software vendor can't blame the data provider when something goes wrong.

If you like the idea of one provider/one payment, the key question is how much power you need for your style of electronic trading. Do you need the capabilities of a corporate trading desk? Or will one of the more limited packages be sufficient for you? You have a wide range of choices of prices and services from which to choose.

Bloomberg

www.bloomberg.com

A Bloomberg machine has established a reputation as a high-powered, top-of-the-line, complete news/information/quotes/analysis service that normally is associated with desktops at the corporate and institutional level. The Bloomberg service seamlessly integrates data, news, analytics, and e-mail into a single platform in one comprehensive service. Users can import Bloomberg data into spreadsheets, process orders through an electronic communications network, do risk analysis, and perform many other trading tasks. Bloomberg Financial Markets delivers information 24 hours a day.

Bridge

www.bridge.com

Bridge, together with its principal operating units—Bridge Information Systems, BridgeNews, Bridge Trading, Savvis, and Telerate—is the largest provider of financial information and related services in North America and the second largest, fastest-growing provider in the world.

Through the use of advanced technology and thanks to a series of strategic acquisitions, Bridge supports a complete range of many different products in its three main business lines: financial information and news products, trading and transaction services, and network services. BridgeNews is one of the world's largest financial news organizations, with more than 600 journalists in 100 countries. Bridge Trading Co. is a full-service stock trading and brokerage firm, and Bridge's technology includes its own high-speed, broadband communications network.

Bridge/CRB MarketCenter Plus

www.crbindex.com

Promoted as two services for the price of one, this package includes CRB/MarketCenter, which includes real-time quotes, news, and charts delivered via the Internet (100 percent Java), and Bridge/CRB PowerSystem, an Internet data service and SystemMaker technical analysis software to create, test, and optimize trading systems. CRBcharts is the next generation in a long line of chart products from Bridge Commodity Research Bureau, which goes back to the first issue of Commodity Chart Service on March 2, 1956. Bridge/CRB DataCenter provides futures and options price data, news stories, technical and fundamental analysis, commentary, and trade recommendations.

CQG

www.cqg.com

Following its entry into the business in 1979, Commodity Quote Graphics, later renamed CQG, soon became a favorite of early electronic traders and has maintained its status among professional traders for its "comprehensive quotes and graphics" and customer service. As a full-service quote vendor, CQG provides real-time prices and analysis for futures, cash markets, and major equities. The standard service fee of $395 per month for individual traders includes a number of technical studies, and you can add a number of sophisticated study packages, news services, and other optional features for additional charges. The Account Tracker function gives detailed information about portfolio holdings and trading activity.

Data Transmission Network Corp. (DTN)

www.dtn.com

An electronic information and communication services provider headquartered in Omaha, NE, DTN offers weather, news, quotes, market analysis, and commentary to one of the largest subscriber bases in the U.S. and Canada via various distribution technologies, most notably satellite delivery. A wide variety of services includes DTN Real-Time, DTN Spectrum (delayed), DTNstant (www.dtnstant.com), DTN Energy (www.dtnergy.com), DTNIQ live stock quotes (www.dtniq.com), DTN AgDayta (www.agdayta .com), and other specialized services targeting agriculture, energy, and other markets. Premium services from other sources are available on dedicated terminals or PC-based services.

Financial Information Management Inc. (ProphetX)

www.fimi.com

This analysis package features a wide variety of futures and options studies, some directed specifically to the energy market. It includes DTN quotes, news, commentary, and weather maps as well as information from Platt's and BridgeNews.

Futurelink Pro

www.futurelinkpro.com

Designed to be a gathering point providing a wide array of news, quotes, charting, and premium services, this site provides some free information, but more advanced services are reserved for members only, including a Java-based charting program, an intraday technical indicator package, analytical commentary, and premium services offered in partnership with leading futures analysts.

FutureSource/Bridge LLC

www.futuresource.com

Professional from FutureSource provides real-time news, prices, analytics, and charting tools in a customizable setting for futures and options. A relatively new version of the original FutureSource package introduced in the 1980s, the emphasis in this version is on speed and drag-and-drop functionality that makes the transfer of data and studies easier. Subscribers can get real-time futures quotes only or a wide variety of analytical and information services at various price levels or specialized add-on services such as Futures World News. Internet PowerPack includes real-time FWN news, delayed futures quotes, intraday options, downloadable ASCII data, expanded charts and studies, time and sales, and weather maps. BridgeChannel is a Java-based financial information application from Bridge Information Systems, delivering current information on global financial markets.

NexTrend Analytical Services Inc.

www.nextrend.com

This subscription service offers U.S. and Canadian exchange data in real-time or snapshot delayed formats. Incorporated in 1993, NexTrend Inc. is the first financial market information provider to create its business and technology specifically to deliver totally integrated market information, professional analysis, and trading services over the Internet. NexTrend Analysis is the core product and includes delayed North American Quotation quotes for $29.95 a month and real-time quotes for $69.95 a month. Enhanced Analysis with more features is $59.95 a month with delayed quotes or $99.95 a month with real-time quotes. NexTrend Electronic Trading enables users to instantly enter electronic trades on direct order-entry systems. NexTrend Trading Models assist in developing optimized trading strategies.

Reuters

www.reuters.com

Reuters is perhaps best known for its long history as a global news organization. The company has added features over the years to become another of the premium trading platform services, frequently found on the desktops at corporations and financial institutions. Reuters Markets 3000 service is the flagship financial information product, covering the money, equity, and fixed-income markets and delivering real-time data, news, and television as well as extensive historical and reference information. Software enables you to display, analyze, and customize information. Commodities 2000 is a comprehensive, screen-based system covering every traded commodity on every exchange in the world as well as cash prices and other information. The specialist Commodities 2000 reporting team is backed up by more than 1800 journalists in more than 140 bureaus and 90 countries. Free futures information is available at www.commods.reuters.com, but you have to register to access the page.

Window on Wallstreet Inc.

www.windowonwallstreet.com

Founded in 1991, Window on WallStreet Inc. (WOW) is an Internet financial solutions company providing online trading tools to traders and investors. As an Internet-enabled "hub" for the online investment community, WOW integrates Financial Data Cast Network (FDCN) with continuously "streaming" financial data, news, and live intraday charts. The Internet Trader Pro 7 Series allows you to scan markets and news, test and rank trading systems, and track portfolios. Day Trader 7 includes the features of Internet Trader Pro plus additional real-time, tick-by-tick analysis capabilities.

FUTURES 'PORTALS'

Some Web sites, including a few of the trading platform products above, are attempting to be the entry point for futures traders on the Internet—a "portal," or the front page from which traders branch out to other sites. They have varying amounts of free information and often have lots of links to other trading-related sites. They focus on generating "hits," since their revenue comes from ad banners or sponsors rather than subscription fees. Some sites are doing a better job than others, but the resources required to launch—and especially maintain—a current, dynamic site make this a challenge. Here are some sites that offer a range of services and connections:

Commoditytrader.net

www.commoditytrader.net

Here you get a smorgasbord of quotes, charts, and news. For quotes, you can pick from what is offered by exchanges, Data Broadcasting Corp., FutureSource, or Quote.com. If the exchange offers real-time quotes, you can get those, but most quotes are delayed 10 minutes, giving you price, time, and size of trades. The site lists about 20 sources for news. Charts are provided by Quote.com.

Commodity Trend Service, or CTS Financial Publishing Inc.

www.ctsinternet.com

The CTS site features TradeWorld2000.com resources for stock and futures traders, such as quotes, charts, indicators, etc. It also includes reports on the TrendSetter trading system and access to fee-based commentary from CTS president Nick Van Nice and a number of other analysts.

Futures.Net

www.futures.net

Touted as a community for futures traders, this site has links to news, quotes, and other resources and carries market commentary and some timeless features from a stable of contributors.

Futuresweb.com

www.futuresweb.com

The Traders Link Directory has numerous links to Web sites and services in more than 40 categories, and Futuresweb has other links to market commentaries, news sources, shopping areas, and many other trader resources.

INO.com

www.ino.com

This investment site launched in March 1995 was one of the first to specialize in futures, options, and forex information, mainly for the individual trader. INO (originally Investment News Online) includes four main segments: (1) QuoteWatch for delayed quotes and charts, (2) MarketCenter for news and resources, such as Futures World News, operated by Bridge, and INO's Exchange News, (3) MarketDepot for shopping, and (4) MarketForum for discussion of trader topics. Entry is free, and no registration is required. INO also offers proprietary products such as GLOBALcharts, OptionsTrader, and iitools.

InvestorLinks.com LLC

www.investorlinks.com/comm.html

www.futureslinks.net

Both of these sites from the same company have links to many other sites in many categories as well as timely research reports and market commentaries updated daily by a number of analysts. Quotes, charts, actively rotating ad banners, and other informative and interesting features keep this lively site fresh.

Site-by-Site!

www.site-by-site.com/usa/optfut.htm

Global and domestic investment information is available on a number of topics, with links in categories such as online trading, quotes and charts, investment newsletters, and so forth. A German version is available.

TFC Commodity Charts

www.tradingcharts.com

This site provides free snapshot quotes and 10-minute delay, with data coming from North American Quotations Inc. The site also has an active forum, a chat room, a training course, bookstore, list of brokers, and more.

Tradehard.com

www.tradehard.com

Essentially an ambitious multifaceted advisory service covering futures and stocks, Tradehard gives you the current thinking of 6 to 12 experts, access to proprietary indicators, news commentaries, how-to-trade forums and articles, and some free items. Membership costs $10 a month, or $95 a year.

Dr. Ed Yardeni's Economics Network

www.yardeni.com

Ed Yardeni, chief economist and global investment strategist of Deutsche Bank Securities in New York, offers some interesting economic commentary, some free and some for a fee. This site is also loaded with links to many financial market and other interesting sites.

PRICE QUOTES

With the growth of the Internet, you can now get some quotes free, although this is still more likely to be true for equities than for futures. Don't overlook what you can get from a broker (see Chapter 3) or the exchanges (see Chapter 4), some of whom provide a significant package of quotes on a real-time, delayed, or snapshot basis. In this section, however, we will assume that you, as an electronic trader, prefer real-time, live, streaming quotes that you can massage with your analytical software and that you will be willing to pay for them.

Quotes come in a variety of forms and prices. A number of services have made the transition to Internet delivery in recent years, putting more emphasis on your choice of a reliable ISP and your connection to the ISP. In those arrangements, the data resides on the data vendor's computers, and you "pull" what you want from the computer when you want it. Essentially, your monthly fee gives you the right to rent the data and manipulate it within the capabilities of the analytical software the company provides or third-party software that you provide.

Other quote services "push" the data to you via satellite or cable services. You own the data and it resides on your computer. You can do whatever you want with it with whatever software you choose. The downside of getting this constant feed of data is when you don't get it. If your computer shuts down or the stream of data is interrupted for any reason, you have no data for the missing period, resulting in gaps in your charts and potentially erroneous calculations in your technical studies or trading systems. In addition, if the flow of data is heavy, you may not receive all the ticks. Occasionally, you also may get bad ticks (exchange or vendor clerical carelessness?) that are so wildly off the mark that they completely distort any chart, technical study, or trading system performance.

You can fill in the gaps and correct the errors with downloads and revisions, of course, but that can be most annoying to an electronic trader who is trying to concentrate on trading.

In any case, you may want to buy historical quotes and subscribe to an end-of-day or real-time delayed quote service in addition to your real-time quotes. Remember, with today's technology, you must think redundancy if good quotes are important to your trading. Buying your own database allows you to backtest your trading ideas and build trading systems with whatever parameters you choose. A daily end-of-day update to your database can provide some comforting insurance that you have—at a relatively low price—backup data that is likely to be more accurate than your real-time data because it has been filtered for errors.

REAL-TIME DATA

Note: Some of the following firms offer services that might place them in other categories. However, they are known primarily as data providers and often supply data for Web sites, firms, or software programs.

Capital Management Sciences (InSite)

www.insite.dbc.com

Real-time market data, news, and research is dynamically updated across all markets for institutional investors and delivered to your PC via the Internet (see Data Broadcasting Corp. below).

Citynet PLC

www.citynet.plc.uk

A streaming data center receives data from various sources and then disseminates it via the Internet to vendors or end-users.

Data Broadcasting Corp. (DBC)

www.dbc.com

As America's leading provider of real-time stock quotes, financial news, and time-sensitive market data, DBC's principal products are marketed and distributed under the Signal, StockEdge, and QuoTrek brand names and under the InSite and BondEdge brand names through its subsidiary Capital Management Sciences, and through MarketWatch.com, its joint venture with CBS.

More than 50 partnerships and alliances offer links to leading financial services and tools for trading, analysis, and portfolio management. eSignal (www.esignal.com) (see Figure 2–1) provides Internet-delivered, real-time, continuously updating market quotes, charts, news, and fundamental data direct to your PC or laptop, as well as delivery via wireless ISP technologies so you can access eSignal online data on the go anywhere. If you have a brokerage account with a firm that supports eSignal's Integrated Trading Solution, you can right-click on a symbol and enter trades directly from the eSignal page.

FIGURE 2–1

Sample Screen from eSignal

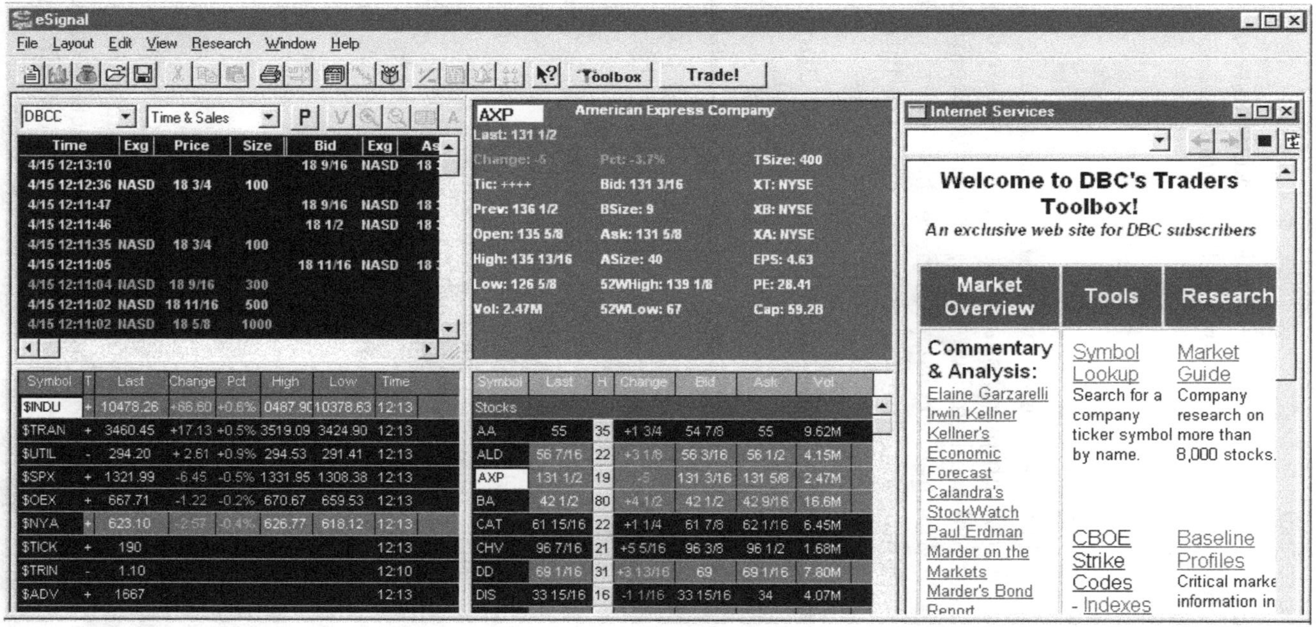

This eSignal screen is an example of what you can receive over the Internet from today's data services. eSignal is loaded with real-time streaming financial data and has links to many more sources, including full-text news and research areas, without leaving the data screen. It can be set up for limit alerts to a pager, a cellular phone or e-mail; for connectivity to major software packages; and for a direct link to your brokerage firm.

Farm Bureau/ACRES

www.acres.fb.com

This basic service offers agricultural market quotes, weather maps, commentary, and news for $19.95 a month.

FutureLink NS

www.futurelinkns.com

The New Standard version offers many customizable features, such as a market hub page, snapshot quotes updated every 10 minutes, technical studies, live news, and radar weather maps from Strategic Weather Service, plus more than a dozen premium services, combining satellite transmission with the Internet.

HyperFeed Technologies Inc. (formerly PC Quote Inc.)

www.pcquote.com

From dynamically updating real-time data to free delayed market data, this company is one of the world's leading providers of online financial information, offering data on more than 350,000 issues from 145 exchanges in 55 countries. HyperFeed 2000 data transmission feed powers all of PC Quote's Internet services. The complete PC Quote 6.0 for Windows package with real-time quotes, charts, Nasdaq Level II, and Turbo options is $300 a month. MarketSmart Real-Time features quotes, news, charting, portfolios, trends, and other data for $9.95 a month, including unlimited real-time quotes for free (subscribers do have to pay fees of their choice for the exchange). MarketSmart Delayed, with 20-minute delay, is free.

Interquote

www.interquote.com

Continuously updating, real-time futures, equities, and options quotes are provided in both spreadsheet and graph formats. Different real-time service levels and fees include tick-by-tick, snapshot, tick-delayed, snapshot-delayed, and end-of-day alternatives. Portfolio evaluation and real-time alerts are included.

Jones Financial Network (PC Trader)

www.pctrader.com

PC Trader offers real-time quotes, news, and analysis from Market News International and several types of charting services, including TradeWind Advanced Charting and Analysis. The core product is $380 a month, but various prices on other packages are available, including just Chicago Board of Trade markets and GovPX Treasury pricing.

Market Research Inc.

www.barchart.com

barchart.com offers a comprehensive futures, commodities, and options service for $20 a month, providing unlimited quotes, charts, custom charts, options analysis, and advanced pages. You can select from a long menu of 250 daily contracts for 50 futures markets or enter a stock symbol and then click on "quote" or "chart" to get free information.

Mobeo Inc. (PocketFutures, F/X Alert, Mobeo 1.0)

www.mobeo.com

Portable real-time quotes and news headlines can be delivered on five different products. Mobeo is a provider of global market information as well as a leader in wireless technology development, delivering real-time quotes on more than 150,000 stocks, options, futures, Treasury, foreign exchange, and other market data.

North American Quotations Inc.

www.naq.com

This real-time quotation service supplies vendors with NAQ development engines and services. NETstream is used by Internet Web service developers to enhance their Web site by providing real-time or delayed stock and futures market information. Internet Real-Time Trader includes an array of technical studies for analysis.

Quote.com

www.quote.com

QCharts 2 service features live, updated charts, customizable quote sheets, technical analysis indicators and charting tools, time and sales data, access to news, research, and analysis. Historical information is stored and updated on the server so you never have to manage data yourself. Multiple Internet server locations route data around bottlenecks. Fees run about $80–$100 per month, depending on the level of service selected, plus exchange fees for real-time quotes.

Standard & Poor's Comstock

www.spcomstock.com

This leading real-time market data provider delivers continuously updated real-time market data, quotes, news, charting, analytics, and other premier services. Coverage includes more than 125 exchanges and sources worldwide, with 256,000 real-time stocks, options, foreign exchange, commodities, and indexes. The basic version is $175 a month, and an enhanced version is $225 a month. Strategic alliances with vendors also provide interfaces with more than 60 third-party software applications. Xpressfeed is a 56KB network with increased bandwidth that ensures you get data delivery and every real-time tick, regardless of data volume and market conditions.

Track Data Corp.

www.tdc.com

Founded in 1981, Track Data Corp. is a major provider of real-time financial market data, financial databases, historical information, analytical services, and data manipulation tools through a private data network to high-end users in equity, options, and futures markets. The company also disseminates news and third-party database information from more than 100 sources worldwide. Its products include MarkeTrack, MarkeTrack 98, ProTrack, myTrack, NewsWare, AIQ Systems, and Dial/Data, offering a range of data services to electronic traders.

END-OF-DAY, HISTORICAL DATA

Brite Futures Inc.

www.britefutures.com

Brite offers free futures charts and price quote pages that can be customized and printed out, or you can download ASCII data to your own software.

Cisco Futures

www.cisco-futures.com

Data can be downloaded in a variety of formats, as can home-study courses and packages for day traders, swing traders, etc.

Commodity Systems Inc. (CSI)

www.csidata.com

CSI offers one of the most extensive historical futures databases, gathering information from more than 50 futures exchanges worldwide. Data for more than 95 percent of the commodities in CSI's inventory extend back to the first day of trading. Data can be purchased on disk in a number of different arrangements, with daily updates available by Internet. Unfair Advantage and Quicktrieve software handle data management and provide some basic charting and analysis tools. CSI also offers MultiMarket Analyzer software, a statistical correlation tool that looks at a collection of user-selected markets from the CSI database and reveals trading opportunities based on correlation, market harmony, and leadership tendencies.

Genesis Financial Data Services

www.gfds.com

Genesis provides end-of-day information on commodities, stocks, options, and mutual funds; tick-by-tick commodities data; and specialty information, such as public sentiment and Commitment of Traders data. Genesis also has tailor-made packages for trading systems and methods such as those used by the Delta Society, Larry Williams, Jake Bernstein, and others.

Glance Market Data Services

www.glancedata.com

This historical database includes Data Master II, a utility program that creates a continuous contract that is updated automatically once it is set up. Its translation engine allows you to create weekly and monthly charts out of your existing daily data.

Logical Information Machines Inc.

www.lim.com

LIM's high-end software performs sophisticated historical equity, bond, and commodity research on an extensive database. Market Information Machine (MIM) software takes complex questions regarding historical commodity, equity, bond, and economic data in near-English without the necessity of any computer programming experience. MIM tests trading rules and simultaneously adds date and time conditions as well as fundamental factors for thorough research.

Pinnacle Data

www.pinnacledata.com

Three databases with updates are available via the Internet. IDX database includes consumer price index, money rates, Federal Reserve rates, etc., with equities back to 1901. CLC database is a historical database of futures prices for 50 commodities, starting in 1969. COT database is a historical database of Commitment of Traders reports, starting in 1983 for most commodities.

Pricecharts.com

www.pricecharts.com

This electronic daily version of Commodity Price Charts gives you updated charts with indicators of your choice for the markets you select. Advisory comments are also available.

Prophet Financial Systems

www.prophetfinance.com

Prophet's Internet site offers both free and subscription-based software applications and information as well as historical financial data and daily market updates for popular PC-based charting systems and spreadsheet programs. Prophet's futures data goes back to 1959, and its index data goes back as far as 1915. There are three different ways to get history and updates online from Prophet: (1) ProphetLink downloading system, which is compatible with almost any PC-based application, (2) ProphetDirect, which gives Omega, MetaStock, and Window on WallStreet users access to data via the downloader already built into the charting software, and (3) FTP or e-mail updates in ASCII files.

Technical Tools

www.techtool.com

TT ChartBook 95 helps you keep your Technical Tools financial database organized and up-to-date with daily updates. You create your own ChartBook, then add pages and arrange them in any order. Drawing tools and analytical functions are available from the TT Library.

Tick Data Inc.

www.tickdata.com

Tick Data, in 1984 the first company in the world to offer historical, tick-by-tick futures prices to personal computer users, has a large database of historical futures, options, and index data. Its data management software allows you to view, plot, or convert tick data into all major analytical formats, including Computrac, Metastock, CSI, and ASCII.

NEWS, PUBLICATIONS, AND OTHER INTERESTING SOURCES

How much news you need for electronic trading will depend on whether you need something other than real-time quotes to make your decisions. You may be one of those traders who only needs to see a chart and price and not necessarily the fundamental factors affecting price movement. Or you may be one of those people who needs to be up-to-date on news events and reports to be comfortable as a trader.

If CNN was the television network of Desert Storm, bringing the bombing of Baghdad into your living room as it happened, then CNBC is the television network for today's generation of active day traders and business news junkies. Television may not provide a great depth of coverage, but CNBC's news reports and expert commentary at least keep active traders in touch with the latest developments that might sway the short-term emotions of the market. At worst, it's just background noise; when something happens, however, it can be a vital alert about something that might move the market.

Television, newspapers, magazines, newsletters, and the like will continue to be vital information sources for traders, but the Internet has become one of the key means of distributing information. In fact, add a "www" and a "dot com" to the name of virtually any publication or television network and you will find a Web site that draws on that source's material in what is essentially a new "online publication."

The Internet is like a vast library offering almost every conceivable form of information. The trick is finding what you want. It is also a great source of disinformation, especially in the news groups and chat pages, where anyone can say anything, so this is a tool that needs to be used with a little discretion. It would be impossible to compile a complete and final list of Internet sites that could provide useful news related to futures trading, because the list is always changing. Following are just a few sources that might be of interest to the electronic futures trader. In some cases, a fee is involved, but many offer free services if you register (and they get your name).

PUBLICATIONS

Together or alone, few names are better known in the news/information/data category than the Dow Jones Company (www.wsj.com) and Reuters News Service (www.reuters.com). Dow Jones publishes *The Wall Street Journal, Barron's,* and a number of news wires, and Reuters has a long history of providing news wire services and data to corporations and financial institutions worldwide. The two news giants announced a joint venture in May 1999 that will provide interactive business services featuring the best information from the archives of both companies (www.bestofboth.com). This site will be able to tap thousands of sources and will offer information in a number of languages.

Both companies have set up extensive Internet operations and will continue to offer their own services independently. That includes *The Wall Street Journal*'s interactive edition (www.interactivewsj.com) and an all-business site (www.dowjones.com), along with a number of specialized sites and regional editions in several languages in addition to the weekly Barron's (www.barrons.com). Reuters will maintain its digital media products. It also offers specialized areas, including one for commodities (www.commods.reuters.com).

Dow Jones is also involved in a joint venture with Hearst Communications on Smart Money (www.smartmoney.com), a portal type of site that contains many investment sources and a 20-minute delayed quote service powered by S&P Comstock.

The New York Times (www.nytimes.com), *Chicago Tribune* (//chicagotribune.com), *U.S.A. Today* (www.usatoday.com), *Investor's Business Daily* (www.investors.com), and many other major newspapers also have active Web sites with business news. So do the television networks, of course—www.msnbc.com/news, www.cbsmarketwatch.com, www.abcnews.go.com, www.cnnfn.com, www.foxnews.com, etc. They tend to be geared to business news of more general interest and to stocks and bonds, but a futures trader should not overlook these as a source of general information.

Futures Magazine

(www.futuresmag.com)

Several articles and reviews from each monthly issue appear online as well as daily updates on hot markets and the technical outlook. What may be most useful on the Futures site are the special issues on specific subjects, such as "Trading as a Business," the annual "Guide to Computerized Trading," and the "SourceBook," which have links to dozens of futures and options industry firms as well as a listing of hundreds of firm names, addresses, phone numbers, and other information.

Technical Analysis of Stocks & Commodities

www.traders.com

Articles here focus on what the monthly magazine's name suggests. There are excerpts from current and past issues online, and a search capability allows you to locate articles that might interest you.

Futures Industry

www.futuresindustry.com

This magazine, published by the Futures Industry Association, tends to be oriented more to broker/exchange issues, but it is very useful for keeping up-to-date on industry matters related to electronic trading and other developments. Complete articles from all issues since 1989 are online and indexed by issue date, author, subject, and title. The site includes a readers' forum to discuss issues affecting the futures industry.

Commodit-e-zine

www.eginc.com/commodit-e-zine

Launched by Earth Group Communications of Omaha in December 1998, this "magazine" is completely online and features articles on various aspects of trading.

TS Express

www.insideedgesystems.com

This "journal for informed users of TradeStation" is published by Inside Edge Systems, which provides tools, programming services, and educational material for Omega Research's TradeStation and SuperCharts. William Brower, president, began providing EasyLanguage programming services full-time in 1993 and began publishing the bimonthly TS Express in January 1994. The company also offers such other services as the DJ Market Timing Service to protect against the downside risk in the stock market.

M. Gordon Publishing Group

www.mgordonpub.com

Related to Tradehard.com (see above), this site offers trading books, software, and research for short-term and day trading, primarily from the work of Jeff Cooper (*Hit and Run Trading* and *5-Day Momentum Method*) and Larry Connors (*Street Smarts* and *Advanced Strategies*).

Bullish Review

www.bullishreview.com

Steve Briese's Web site provides Commitment of Traders data, which he analyzes and interprets in his newsletter service using his proprietary CoT Indexes.

Club 3000

www.ison.com/club3000/index.html

This network of commodity traders has been operating since 1981, discussing all aspects of trading. Comments tend to focus on—but are not limited to—trading systems and their performance. The club has more than 1000 members on five continents. Most communication is via a print newsletter. Text search facilities exist to search an extensive database of past articles, if you want to see what members have to say about a system before you buy it.

Commodity Traders Club News

www.webtrading.com

Traders share information about trading tactics, software, and whatever else interests them.

Futures Truth Co.

www.futurestruth.com

Futures Truth provides an independent analysis of trading systems traded, just as if a customer opened the box and began trading a system. If a system's parameters can be programmed and followed objectively, that system can be tested by Futures Truth, which publishes the trading results in great detail and ranks systems according to performance.

Pinson Communications

www.publicationsetc.com

This subscription service offers trading publications of many types.

ZDNet Anchor Desk

www.zdnet.com/anchordesk

This online computer publication is not connected to trading, but if you want to keep up on the latest developments in computers, software, data transmission, or other technology issues, this site covers it and gives you links for more information.

Traders Library

www.traderslibrary.com

This online bookstore has an active Web site offering books, videos, audiotapes, newsletters, and more on many topics related to investing and trading. You can search by title, by author, or by category to find books that interest you.

Traders Press Inc.

www.traderspressbookstores.com

In addition to offering the usual range of trading books, this company is also known for reprinting or carrying some of the classic trading books of the past that are difficult to find in most bookstores.

OTHER INFORMATION SOURCES

The following list includes only a few of the hundreds of advisory services available as well as a number of other sites that might interest an electronic trader. The sites are listed in no particular order.

Listen Only Squawk Box

www.los.net

This service describes the action—ringside—in the S&P 500 Index pit, verbally, from bell to bell, giving you a feel for the moods on the trading floor.

Intersat Space Communications Corp.

www.intersat.com

PitWarrior Audio is the information service designed to provide the very fastest bell-to-bell commentary related to the action in the S&P 500 futures contract. Dedicated to this task and nothing else, PitWarrior provides bids, offers, trades, major size, and the perpetrators, documenting what the locals are up to and where the paper is coming from. It's an alternative to just waiting for your quote screen to report prices after the fact. This real-time service is only available via the satellite broadcast services of InterSat, which offers a full range of high-speed data, audio and video transmission services, and live audio broadcasts from exchange floors.

AgriWeather

www.agriweather.com

In this joint venture with FutureSource Bridge, AccuWeather provides a free one-stop site focusing on weather of interest to agricultural traders. Type in a zip code or city and you get various types of maps, forecasts, and other weather information. The site also offers access to FutureSource Bridge news by keyword, price quotes, and charts.

Commodity Timing

www.ctiming.com

Legendary trader Larry Williams' advisory service uses mechanical trading systems and proven trading strategies to isolate trades recommended nightly by hotline, fax, or e-mail, and in a monthly newsletter that includes reports on new trading strategies and systems.

Linda Raschke

www.mrci.com/lbr

One of the futures industry's best-known traders demonstrates how she trades real-time in live, online trading.

Tom Jackson's DayTrader

www.sp-daytrade.com

This subscription-based service uses the Internet to give you an "early morning special" in Dow Jones and S&P 500 Index futures. You pay $10 for each winning trade, nothing for a losing trade.

Sunny Harris & Associates Inc.

www.moneymentor.com

This firm specializes in various educational, consulting, and mentoring services and publishes the Traders' Catalog & Resource Guide. The Web site offers news, quotes, and links to many resources.

DayTrader Corporation

www.wealthytrader.com

Todd Mitchell offers a training course and personal mentoring to teach people how to trade the S&P 500 Index.

First Internet National Directory (FIND)

www.findbrokers.com

The FIND Commodity Brokers Directory has links to many sources in three dozen categories, plus some broker profiles (with photos).

Commodity Central

www.commoditycentral.com

The site from Autumn Investments of Greenville, TN, features "Mikey's Methods," with free-wheeling comments on many aspects of trading, a training course, paper trading, and the Commodity Cafe forum, among other things.

SMOTASS

www.smotass.net

Successful Methodical Online Traders Accessing Speculative Sites has one of the most extensive lists of futures and options Web sites, which cover more than 20 categories.

Waldemar's List

www.netservers.com/~waldemar/list.shtml

Waldemar Puszkarz's collection of links to futures sites on the Internet includes dozens of links in a number of categories for futures traders and is updated occasionally.

Institute of Finance and Banking at the University of Göttingen

www.wiso.gwdg.de/ifbg/finfut.html

The link listed here is to a page of links to various futures trading sites, but the institute also has numerous other links to sites related to finance, banking, currencies, and more.

Traders Auction

www.tradersauction.com

New and used trading tools are offered in auction format as a service of Commodity Traders Club News.

About.com Inc.

http://economics.about.com

http://daytrading.about.com

About.com has lots of links on lots of general subjects, including several pages specifically targeting trading. Only two pages are listed here, but they can lead to many resources.

Institutional Advisory Services Group (IASG)

www.iasg.com

IASG provides European and American institutional, brokerage, and high net-worth individual futures market participants with professional access to the world's futures and foreign exchange markets. A comprehensive managed futures investment chart site on the Internet offers free monthly historical charts and research on 100 trading advisors, funds, and hedge funds. Although this may not seem like the type of service usually associated with electronic trading, the IASG 100 Managed Futures Report and Top 30 Rankings may be part of a different type of online research that can help make the difference when trading futures and options.

Investment Reference

www.irfutures.com

Dennis Stahr provides consulting services in a number of areas, such as preparing for the Series 3 futures exam and several securities exams, developing disclosure documents, registering and setting up commodity trading advisor or introducing broker operations, internal field audits, and the like. His Web site also includes useful articles and answers to questions from traders.

FACS Journalists' Guide to Economic Terms

www.facsnet.org/report_tools/guides_primers/
glossary.htm

Even if you're not a journalist, here's a glossary to help you sort through today's economic lingo.

ORGANIZATIONS, REGULATORS, GOVERNMENT

Futures Industry Association (FIA)

www.fiafii.org

FIA is the only association representative of all organizations that have an interest in the futures market and includes more than 200 corporate members. The futures commission merchant members are responsible for an estimated 80 percent or more of the customer business transacted on U.S. futures exchanges. In addition to information about the association in the FIA section, the site includes a "yellow pages" section with listings and links for many firms. Active traders may be especially interested in the Futures Industry Institute (FII) section, with its educational services and the constantly updated Fact Book, which has exchange, contract, and other useful reference information online, on disk, or in print.

International Federation of Technical Analysts

www.ifta.org

IFTA is an international nonprofit professional organization of market analysis societies and associations, with members in 26 countries. Incorporated in 1986, its goals include providing a centralized international exchange for information, data, business practices, local customs, and all matters related to technical analysis in various financial centers. One of its member associations is the Market Technicians Association in the United States (see next item).

Market Technicians Association

www.mta-usa.org

MTA, incorporated in 1973, is a not-for-profit organization of market analysis professionals in the United States. Its goals are to encourage the exchange of technical information and collectively explore new frontiers in the area of technical research; educate the public and the investment community about the use, value, and limitations of technical research; and uphold a code of ethics and professional standards among technical analysts. MTA services include publications, an annual conference, and a certification program.

The Office for Futures and Options Research

www.aces.uiuc.edu/ACE/ofor/new.html

The Office for Futures and Options Research (OFOR) at the University of Illinois at Urbana-Champaign promotes and enhances scholarly research and learning regarding futures, options, and derivative markets. It bridges the teaching and research programs of the Department of Agricultural and Consumer Economics and the Department of Finance. OFOR seeks to improve the understanding, information, and economic knowledge base of futures, options, and derivative markets and then to disseminate this improved knowledge to other scholars, users, practitioners, regulators, and students of these markets. This is another source that may not catch the eye of short-term electronic traders, but it offers many papers, views, and comments that may be useful. The material is academic and some of it deals with agriculture and hedging.

Commodity Floor Brokers and Traders Association (CFBTA)

www.cfbta.org

The CFBTA's Futures Industry Products and Services Guide has links to hundreds of useful products and services for traders.

National Futures Association (NFA)

www.nfa.futures.org

This U.S. self-regulatory organization's mission is to protect the rights of investors in futures markets. The NFA is responsible for registering brokers, trading advisors, etc., and its site has a button labeled "BASIC"—Background Affiliation Status Information Center—providing information about futures "professionals" that might be particularly useful to anyone trying to check the record of a firm or individual in the futures industry.

Commodity Futures Trading Commission (CFTC)

www.cftc.gov

The home page of the federal regulatory agency for U.S. futures trading includes links to other government sites, timely updates on all the agency's latest regulatory developments, the Commitments of Traders data, and other reports.

Securities and Exchange Commission (SEC)

www.sec.gov

The U.S. securities regulator provides information on current regulatory developments, the EDGAR database, and other matters related to the securities business.

U.S. Federal Reserve Board

www.bog.frb.fed.us

Everybody knows the significance of "the Fed" on U.S. monetary policy and the impact its decisions can have on interest rate and stock index contracts.

Bureau of Economic Analysis

www.bea.doc.gov/beahome.html

This agency of the U.S. Department of Commerce is the nation's economic accountant, preparing estimates that illuminate key national, international, and regional aspects of the U.S. economy and producing lots of economic data.

U.S. Department of Agriculture (USDA)

www.usda.gov

The USDA is the source of many key reports affecting traders and has a treasure of current and historical data in its archives—if the site's search engines can lead you where you want to go.

National Agricultural Statistics Service (NASS)

www.usda.gov/nass

NASS is only one of many USDA agencies online, but it's a key one because it is the source of many of the major government reports that have an impact on agricultural markets.

Can't figure out where to find something among the U.S. government's millions of pages of information available on the Internet? Try www.usgovsearch.com from Northern Light Technology LLC. It will cost you $5 a day (or $30 a month, or $250 a year) to use this search engine site, but it may be worth it to get to the information you want more quickly.

FORUMS, CHATS, NEWSGROUPS

One of the most interesting aspects of the Internet—and often the most misused and abused—is its capacity to allow traders to find and talk to each other via bulletin board services, forums, chat rooms, newsgroups, and so forth. A number of sites offer a forum as one of their services, and their popularity runs hot and cold as traders shift from one to the other, depending on the topic, the markets, etc.

Some are moderated, which puts a filter on the content, but others are free-flowing, "freedom of speech" at its best—or worst. The newsgroups, in particular, tend to be a mix of informative items, helpful tips, blatant promotional material, ego ranting and raving, flaming, and spamming. The trader who has time to scan these resources and select the nuggets from the disinformation can get some useful insights or answers to questions from some of the best minds in the business. However, you might want to be cautious or skeptical about the input and responses you get from these services.

The long list of newsgroups is always expanding, as almost any topic seems to inspire a newsgroup. Among those that might interest futures traders are the long-established misc.invest groups: **misc.invest.forex, misc.invest.futures, misc.invest .commodities, misc.invest.technical**, or **misc.invest.options**. You can also search the Usenet news archives with Deja News (**www.dejanews.com**) to find topics, contributors, and other information.

Avid Traders Chat

www.avidtrader.com/chat

Advisory comments and free trader's chat features guest experts.

Commodity Café

www.commoditycafe.com

This is an active and snappy talk forum portion of Commodity Central, with most of the comments and observations about market prospects.

Soft Trade Inc.

www.softtradeinc.com

In addition to a forum, this site includes free charts and links.

Marketforum.com

www.marketforum.com

This active INO.com forum site gets 300 to 400 messages per day on a variety of market topics.

Real Traders

www.realtraders.com

Topics tend to be related to software and systems.

Silicon Investor

www.techstocks.com

This financial discussion site includes forums for specific types of trading, plus a number of other useful links.

omega-list@eskimo.com

This bulletin board service is not sponsored by Omega Research but has many comments and tips on Omega and related technical analysis products. It includes some of the sharpest, most helpful traders in any of the forums.

ANALYTICAL SOFTWARE

If everything you need for your electronic trading program is provided by a broker or by one of the trading platforms described above, you may not need to review this section on software that can help you with your pretrade analysis. On the other hand, you may want to use additional analytical tools or you may want to refine what you can do by applying a specialized concept to the data you have. In that case, you may be interested in one of the hundreds of stand-alone analytical software programs available to futures traders.

In particular, you may want to put your own or someone else's ideas into a mechanical trading system, and you may want to know how this system would have fared if you had used it in the past. For example, visually, on a chart, a moving average system might look like it did very well, but what does the history of actual profits and losses show? Is the moving average you selected the best one? What kind and size of stop should you use with your system? What amount of drawdown can you expect with this system, and can you cope with it?

That is the type of analysis you can do with the "toolbox programs," which allow you to write and test trading systems from scratch to find a strategy that works. But as one vendor of another type of software contends on its Web page, "This [type of research] can be a very time-consuming and unrewarding endeavor for most people. Imagine being given hundreds of tools to build a house but not having any plans to work from or training on how each tool works. Unless you're a professional trading system developer by trade, these toolbox programs probably aren't the solution for you."

Electronic traders who do have some skills with a computer and investing may not be satisfied with an alternative on the other end of the scale either, the "black-box" canned systems. They involve no analysis at all, other than picking the "right" system. These programs give you exact trading signals but no clear indication as to how the signals were generated—and usually no confidence to stay with the system if market conditions change and the system has a few losses.

Somewhere in between are the "gray box" or "white box" systems, which disclose some or all of their features, and the technical analysis packages, which produce charts and indicators of various types to help you analyze markets, but also let you draw your own subjective conclusions when it comes to trading decisions.

You have to gear what you need to your style of trading. On the one hand, it seems like you can never have enough analysis as the market gyrates around. On the other hand, it is easy to fall into the "analysis paralysis" trap—overanalyzing to the point that you can't pull the trigger on a trade. "Sometimes, when you have all the toys, you don't learn how to trade. You learn how to work the toys but not how to trade," contends Larry Rosenberg, who uses his laptop "office in a box" for his trading and prefers to stick with the simpler trading tools.

A WORD ABOUT TRADING SYSTEMS

When it comes to trading, probably nothing could be more exciting to most people than to have a system that "beats the market"—that consistently buys low and sells high or vice versa. You not only rake in big profits but you also have the satisfaction of "being right." The Holy Grail system has been the dream of traders probably since trading began. The difference today is that software is available that can help you in this quest... although it still can't deliver the Holy Grail.

If you have a trading method that you can explain in specific terms, chances are good that one of today's computer programming languages can turn your ideas into trading rules. These rules, in turn, can be put together to produce a trading system. That, essentially, is what the system software vendors have done for you, presenting you with their techniques in the black-box systems, which only give you the end-result trading signals, or in a gray-box program, which allows you to tweak a parameter or two.

A few programs let you design your own system from start to finish and go beyond that by letting you backtest the system over past data. These programs give you the ability to optimize parameters to come up with those that produce the best result, whether you think of that as total profit, percentage of winning trades, least drawdown—whatever criteria you think is most important. Whether you purchase a trading system or develop a system of your own that looks promising, you should keep in mind that system results can be very deceptive, depending on the number of parameters, how the parameters have been fit to the data, and the time period being analyzed, among other things. Hypothetical results used to promote some systems may not be possible in real-world trading, so it pays to be a little skeptical about any trading system and to understand it thoroughly before you trade it.

The big advantage of system development software is that you can test virtually any trading idea that can be programmed and get an idea of what your results might be without risking a penny in the marketplace. You can use the canned techniques provided, modifying their parameters, or you can write your own systems and then see how they would have fared on actual data.

How much money did the system make? How many of the trades were winners? What was the largest drawdown? What was the profit per trade? What size and type of stops should you use? You can get those answers in seconds with a system development program. If you don't like what you see with a five-day moving average system, for example, try six days. If your drawdown is too large with a $600 stop, change the stop to $400. Or tell the computer to optimize the system and show you the best combination of parameters for the time period you specify.

In short, trading system development software can be a very useful and powerful tool that can guide your trading onto the right track. Traders should be aware, however, that this software needs to be used with care before relying on it too heavily. One of the dangers is that just because the software is so sophisticated and can do it, you might have a tendency to over-optimize or curve-fit the parameters to the data. When you can keep refining your program until you get results that appeal to you, keep in mind that a system that performs well on past data may not be able to maintain that record in current or future market conditions.

Traders should also be aware of several other features of system development software. A common instruction in a system may be something like, "If X occurs, then buy this bar on the close." Until you have the close, you don't know you have a signal. By then, of course, you may not be able to make a trade at that signal price because the market is closed, even though the system says you made a trade and bases its results on a trade at that price. If the next bar gaps many points away from where the trade was signaled, it may look like you have a huge profit when you aren't even in the market.

The same type of problem arises when the instruction is, "Buy the next bar on the open." The system may show you long on a day the market locked limit up and it was impossible for you to have even gotten a position. Following its instructions literally, the system may show it was positioned long for a big runup on the one big trade that accounts for most of the system's profits, when in reality, you were left sitting on the sidelines or you entered the market at a far different point than the system software indicates.

In backtesting, system development software also doesn't know the order in which ticks occurred in a given bar: Did the high or the low occur first? Could you have acted on a signal, or did prices occur in a pattern that would have made following the system impossible? That may be very significant to an electronic trader trying to use a short-term trading system.

None of this is intended to negate the value of software that can develop and test trading systems, but you need to analyze the system results as much as you analyze the market. Used blindly, you may be quite surprised if your actual results are far different from your theoretical results. Used properly, system development software can be a great tool for taking full advantage of the power of your computer to find profitable trading methods that you might never have spotted visually.

ANALYTICAL SOFTWARE

The following list includes all types of software for technical analysis. Most listings are by company name, but in some cases, the name of the software product may be better known and is in parentheses. As with the data services above, we emphasize again that it is impossible to make any list of trading software complete and comprehensive and current. Some listings may be directed more to equities trading or may be better suited to end-of-day data than to a day trading time frame. And a few listings are not software at all but offer computer-related help for the electronic futures trader.

The software programs are generally stand-alone products that can be used to analyze futures data, can usually be applied to a number of data feeds, function in real-time situations, and have an Internet site so you can further check them out yourself. (Our assumption is that if the firm is serious about attracting electronic traders, it probably has an Internet marketing site.)

The most important thing about software is that it fit what you are trying to do. For many electronic traders willing to pay an ongoing monthly fee for real-time quotes and analysis, the trading platform services would probably cover about everything those traders would want to do. But if you are a chart watcher who only needs data and a basic charting program, you may prefer not paying for that kind of service. Or you may be the kind of trader who requires the discipline of a mechanical trading system and has time to tinker with lots of ideas to produce exact entry and exit points. Or perhaps you are one of those traders who just likes to try every piece of software that comes along.

There is no one right way to trade. Electronic trading implies short-term thinking, but numerous trading styles are possible within that time frame. Know what kind of trader you are, then select the software that makes your job easier or enhances your trading ability.

FIGURE 2-2

Omega Research—ProSuite 2000i

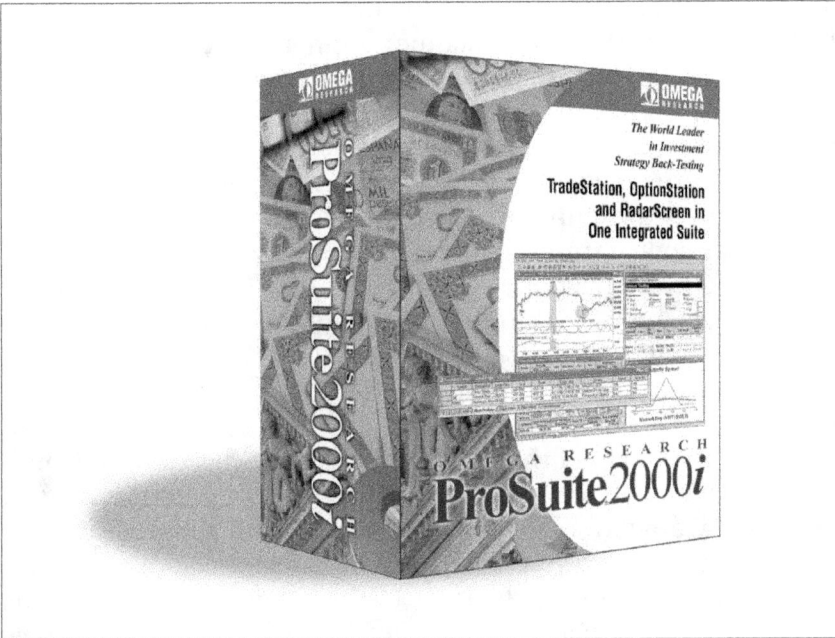

ProSuite 2000i is Omega Research's product for the new millenium, combining such new features as RadarScreen 2000i with the capabilities that made TradeStation, OptionStation, and SuperCharts the leading analytical software programs of the 1990s.

Omega Research Inc.

www.omegaresearch.com

Because a number of the following software programs are based on products offered by Omega Research, we are starting our list of analytical software with Omega, one of the best-known suppliers of software for individual traders since it was founded by brothers Bill and Ralph Cruz in Miami in 1982. Omega's first major product was SystemWriter, an end-of-day program introduced a week before the stock market crash in 1987. Then came TradeStation in 1991, designed to analyze data in real-time, SuperCharts, both end-of-day and real-time versions, and in 1996, OptionStation.

In 1999 Omega introduced a new series of products that can be purchased either individually or together as ProSuite 2000i. TradeStation 2000i builds on its reputation of being the standard in developing and testing system trading software and now features SystemBuilder, a modular approach to building trading systems. RadarScreen 2000i is a new product that scans the market in real-time to find stocks that meet the user's customizable criteria, ranking and sorting them as the user chooses. OptionStation 2000i finds and tracks option positions based on user assumptions. Omega also launched **historybank .com** to provide data for historical testing.

TradeStation 2000i, RadarScreen 2000i, and OptionStation 2000i are each priced (currently) at $2399, or you can purchase the ProSuite package with everything for $4799. Those upgrading from earlier versions of Omega products pay a somewhat lower price.

The attraction of the Omega products is that they give individuals with a personal computer the capability to create, modify, and test trading systems in the same way that sophisticated institutional traders can do with their mainframe computers. With Omega's *Easy Language* feature, traders can convert their ideas into trading rules using common words without having to know a complex programming language.

Although the Omega products have their shortcomings, they have been at the forefront in enhancing electronic trading in the 1990s. They even spawned a number of cottage industries, as the so-called Omega Solution Providers produced trading systems and add-on products that are well-represented throughout the list below. You can check the Omega Web site or Omega Research magazine for a complete current list of solution providers.

AbleSys Corp. (ASCTrend)

www.ablesys.com

This universal indicator package focuses on identifying trends and spotting trend changes early for any market in any time frame.

AIQ Systems (TradingExpert Pro)

www.aiq.com

This system development program uses artificial intelligence techniques. It is available with the myTrack real-time data service from Track Data Corp. for a monthly fee.

ARC Systems Inc.

www.trendpro.com

Roy Kelly Futures and Stocks Service offers the TrendPro indicators package for all versions of TradeStation and SuperCharts, and an advisory service provides trade recommendations intraday by e-mail, fax, or pager.

Aspen Graphics

www.aspenres.com

The Aspen database engine for extensive real-time market analysis uses provided studies or you can write your own to configure your charts and analyze markets. The 32-bit Windows application handles most major data feeds.

Walter Bressert Futures Online

www.walterbressert.com

In addition to advisory services and seminars, Walter Bressert offers ProfitTrader 5.0 cycle trading software developed by Bressert and Roy Kelly and designed to fit any market and any time frame.

CA-NI Industries Ltd. (Wisdom of the Ages)

www.caniindustries.com

CA-NI's computer algorithms are designed to run on TradeStation and combine 10 trading rules for a trading system best suited for 1-minute bars.

Cablesoft Inc. (LiveWire)

www.livewire-cablesoft.com

This online integrated investment software monitors the market, analyzes charts, and provides portfolio management tick by tick.

Choice Daytrades

www.choicedaytrades.com

These day trading and technical analysis tools for the S&P 500 Index are designed for users of Omega Research products.

Clayburg Custom Programming (Cyclone System)

www.pionet.net/~clayburg

A longer-term day trading system is based on support/resistance points from several previous sessions.

Coast Investment Software Inc.

www.fibtrader.com

Joe Dinapoli's Fibonacci and other studies calculate support/resistance points and update these calculations on a real-time data feed.

COMMODEX

www.commodex.com

The oldest, most diversified daily trading system for futures incorporates price, volume, and open interest. Subset portfolios can be based on account size.

ConNETics Technology Group

www.coa-trading.com

Trading systems and trading tools are designed for day trading the S&P 500 and Nasdaq 100 indexes, bonds, and currencies using TradeStation.

Creative Breakthrough Inc.

www.futures-cbi.com

CBI offers systems for S&P 500 Index day trading as well as a suite of position-trading systems for various markets.

Dynacomp Inc.

www.dynacompsoftware.com

Dynacomp offers a wide range of software products by interactive catalog.

DynaStore

www.freeyellow.com/members6/dynastorelight/
index.html

The DynaStore from Power Forex Software serves as a data manager emulator and allows programs such as Omega TradeStation 2000i and Equis MetaStock Pro 6.52 to connect to a variety of data sources beyond those programmed by Omega and Equis.

Ehrlich Commodity Futures

www.stanehrlich.com

Ehrlich Cycle Forecaster is an add-on to Omega Research products that shows cyclical price rhythms for any chart.

Ensign Software

www.ensignsoftware.com

This charting software uses DTN, BMI, or eSignal data feeds and contains numerous technical studies and drawing features for a monthly fee. It also provides access to news, weather maps, and other services.

Equis International Inc. (MetaStock)

www.equis.com

MetaStock Professional is a toolbox type of program available in several versions from Equis, a Reuters company. It can produce a full range of technical analysis charts and studies and performs system tests, data searches, and more. Traders can create, test, optimize, and fully automate trading systems with such features as flexible charting, a complete collection of trading indicators, and expert advisory comments.

Essex Trading Co. Ltd.

www.essextrading.com

Futures Pro and Option Pro proprietary trading strategies have specific buy/sell signals for most global futures markets or can be used as a toolbox for historical testing.

Financial Facilitators

www.finf.com

Systems for S&P 500 Index and Dow Jones Industrial Average futures are based on short-term trends and have initial and annual license fees.

Futures Conferences Ltd. (Computrade)

www.fcltd.com

Computrade Intraday Range Forecaster calculates daily support/ resistance numbers for day trading.

GlobalView Software Inc.

www.gvsi.com

This database software distributes and displays real-time and historical market information. The open architecture design supports multiple users and numerous configurations.

Institute for Options Research (Option Master)

www.options-inc.com

Ken Trester's options analysis site offers a number of free resources plus software, training videos, and courses.

International Trading Systems (The Collective)

www.internationaltrading.com

This collection of proprietary-designed, fully automated, "white box" mechanical trading systems features prices based on a system's performance. Among the programs offered is WinWaves 32 for Elliott Wave analysis.

Investment Engineering Corp.

www.investlabs.com

These add-on "power tools" for Trade Station and SuperCharts include specialized programs for system developers and ways to view quotes and convert text to speech.

Investorsoftware.com

www.investorsoftware.com

Anderson Investor's Software in St. Louis distributes numerous investment software programs via the Internet.

Investors Technical Services (Behold!)

www.bhld.com

Most analysis software is limited to PCs, but this is a Macintosh program to develop and optimize almost any trading system. You can write your own indicators and trading rules and test and optimize portfolios.

IRIS

www.iris.nl

Three decision-support systems analyze futures and options and manage positions and portfolios. A data feed supplies real-time data. Products include Rubyx for LIFFE CONNECT for futures, an application for trading on electronic exchanges, and The

Futures & Options Trader (TFOT), providing all the main utilities and management capabilities of a market maker.

Kase & Co. Inc.

www.kaseco.com

This trading and hedging advisory firm normally supports only corporate and institutional clients, primarily in the energy sector, but it offers some programs to private investors, including Kase StatWare, an indicator library containing momentum and risk management algorithms.

Joe Krutsinger Inc.

www.joekrut.com

An Omega Research solution provider, Joe Krutsinger is a system development consultant who has helped some of the world's best traders transform their trading ideas into computer-based systems. He also sells systems and books and offers private seminars.

Leading Market Technologies (EXPO)

www.lmt-expo.com

This is an advanced analytics and decision-support platform for professional traders, analysts, and portfolio managers. EXPO add-in modules include EXPO/Econometrics to apply econometric techniques to real-time market data and EXPO/Monte Carlo to integrate the power of Monte Carlo simulation into analysis. MarketBrowser provides point-and-click access to Reuters, the Bloomberg service, Logical Information Machines, and many other popular data sources.

Linn Software Inc. (Investor/RT)

www.linnsoft.com

This investment software tracks and filters large databases, offering real-time advanced charting, technical analysis, and custom indicators for day traders using Windows or Power Mac.

Market Technologies Corp. (Vantage Point)

www.profittaker.com

This software for financial futures markets includes technical analysis, intermarket analysis, neural networks, moving averages, and price forecasts.

McMillan Analysis Corp.

www.optionstrategist.com

Larry McMillan offers short-term stock and options strategies and techniques and other resources for options traders.

Mesa Software Inc.

www.mesasoftware.com

John Ehlers offers a series of cyclical analysis software programs for various time frames including R-Mesa for S&P 500 day trading and Sierra Hotel for Japanese yen trading.

Meyers Analytics LLC

www.meyersanalytics.com

Dennis Meyers presents advanced short-term and intraday systems and indicators compatible with TradeStation. His algorithms use Kalman and Polynomial filters and End Point Fast Fourier Transform.

Micro Media (Moon Tide)

www.cashinonchaos.com

Hans Hannula researches chaos in financial markets to produce market timing services linking emotional swings in markets to tides in the earth's electric field. Mathematical models forecast price swings.

MicroStar Research and Trading Inc.

www.microstar-research.com

MicroStar's trading systems include Top Step, based on intraday market and price patterns in interest rates, indexes, and currencies.

Mindfire Systems

www.mindfire-systems.com

Trading systems from Randy Stuckey include Catscan, featuring a choppiness index, Golden SX, and Millennium 2000, a reversal system.

National Trading Group Inc.

www.ntg-futures.com

Ned Gandevani developed the Winning Edge S&P 500 Index day trading methodology based on chaos theory fundamentals and years of observation and research.

NetTraderRT

www.mxcapital.com

This technical analysis/charting application uses real-time data from Quote.com. You can write, backtest, optimize, and automate your own trading systems and indicators or use and modify the tools provided. "Genetic optimization" saves time by using artificial intelligence to find the best parameters without having to try every combination. You can set up a direct connection to your online broker to place trades and get news.

Nirvana Systems Inc. (Omni Trader)

www.omnitrader.com

This automated market analysis program comes with 120 trading systems built in and uses adaptive reasoning technology to adapt to the current personality of each market to produce trading signals.

NPA Futures Inc.

www.talkingtools.com

Day Traders Talking Toolbox acts as a trader's assistant to convert certain chart patterns and other occurrences in TradeStation or SuperCharts into indicators and alerts announced by a female voice.

Option Wizard Online

www.option-wizard.com

The Microsoft Excel spreadsheet program is used to price puts and calls.

OptionsAnalysis.com

www.optionsanalysis.com

This Web-based analysis and trade-finding service includes daily tables of expensive and cheap options. Historical options data for futures goes back to May 1995.

Option Dynamics

www.aros.net/~options

These programs evaluate options on equities, indexes, and futures.

Optionetics

www.optionetics.com

Education and software for a variety of option strategies developed by George Fontanills emphasizes reduced risk and low stress for off-floor traders.

Optionomics Corp. (Orion Risk Management System)

www.optionomics.com

This is a premium risk management and options analytical suite for a variety of systems, including real-time data and portfolio management.

OptionVue Systems International Inc.

www.optionvue.com

OptionVue provides a complete array of analysis tools for the options trader, from software to seminars. NetVue provides Internet access to databases, and OpScan searches for trading opportunities.

Profitunity Trading Group

www.profitunity.com

Bill Williams offers Investor's Dream trading software, which produces proprietary entry/exit signals and exact orders to give your broker as well as a home study course and trading tutorials.

Promised Land Technologies Inc.

www.promland.com

Braincel (add-in to Excel) and FuturesBuilder use neural net technology to develop forecasting applications and "mine" data for hidden links and relationships.

Reinhart Investment Management

www.betterjob.com/ar.html

The Action/Reaction Course and software are based on the works of Dr. Alan Hall Andrews and Roger Babson, who applied natural law to predict market behavior.

Rina Systems

www.rinasystems.com

This performance analysis software allows you to create and historically test entire portfolios of trading systems and markets, revealing combinations that have superior performance.

Ruggiero Associates

E-mail: 71054.3545@compuserve.com

Murray Ruggiero develops trading system software, focusing on TradeStation and Excel, and writes numerous articles and publications on the topic.

S&P Scalper Software

home.earthlink.net/~sptrader

Scalper software is not a trading system that tells you when and where to trade but rather a real-time indicator of possible trend reversals for day trading S&P 500 Index futures.

SirTrade International (SAFIR-X)

www.sirtrade.com

Pierre Orphelin offers the assistant for expert traders, including technical analysis and automated trading systems, advanced artificial intelligence and neurofuzzy logic tools, and applications and adaptive neurofuzzy systems for real-time trading.

Software Solutions (Entrypoint 2000i)

www.softwaresolutions-inc.com

Educational and decision-support software provides main trend and mid-trend indicators, a trend strength index, and alerts for potential trades.

Stoll Momentum System Inc.

www.fxfx.com

This analysis method studies the rate of change in prices over time. Various models identify trend changes and make timing recommendations to complement other analysis.

TechHackers

www.thi.com

TechHackers offers Intelligent Financial Systems analytic programming modules, spreadsheet add-ins, real-time data, and consulting services.

THA Inc. (Drummond Geometry)

www.tedtick.com

This computerized training course can be applied to trading any time frame and has indicators for TradeStation.

Tierra del Fuego Ltd.

www.tdfltd.com

This site supplies financial software and daily reports.

Titan Trading Analytics (Virtual Trader)

www.titantrading.com

Titan develops short-term financial trading systems using VirtualTrader, its TradeStation-based trading simulator, and provides training services for private and professional traders.

Top Gun Trading Systems Inc.

www.acinvestments.com

A.C. Investments offers day trading signals from the proprietary Top Gun system for trading the most popular currency markets and T-bonds.

Trader's Edge

www.tradersedge.com

This Canadian-based Windows program is designed to track investment portfolios and provide reports that meet Canadian tax requirements.

Traders Software Co. Inc. (TSCI)

www.futurestrades.com or www.futureslinks.com

Michael A. Mermer offers a computerized trading program, ETS, for Omega Research's TradeStation and SuperCharts and is publisher of the ETS Real-Time Trading Advisory, published live on the Internet and by fax, with recommendations on stock indexes and bonds.

Trader's Toolbox

www.janarps.com

Omega Solution Provider Jan Arps offers many add-on indicators and systems for TradeStation and SuperCharts as well as custom Easy Language programming.

TraderWare X

www.markbrown.com

This toolbox software to customize program studies and develop trading systems uses various programming languages.

TradeSignals.com

www.tradesignals.com

These professional futures trading strategies include an S&P 500 E-mini day trading system as well as systematic analysis of more than 50 futures markets daily.

TradeStorm Inc.

www.tradestorm.com

Storm is an automated strategy for trading S&P futures, using a concept similar to support and resistance but including a breakout component and a stop-loss equal to $700. Programmed for Omega TradeStation and SuperCharts Real-Time, it is available for informational purposes or by lease.

Trade System Inc. (Aberration)

www.trade-system.com

This trading system uses the same rules and parameters on all markets, adjustable to account size.

Trading Systems International Inc.

www.tradeintl.com

This series of trading programs for TradeStation and SuperCharts combines trend and breakout concepts to identify major market moves designed for high average win/loss ratios.

Trading Technologies

www.tradingtechnologies.com

An integrated trading software suite provides a fast, adaptable interface for sophisticated traders, brokers, and risk managers. Various software modules include a real-time position manager, flexible automatic quoting system, and an order-routing system.

Trading Techniques Inc. (Advanced GET)

www.tradingtech.com

This comprehensive set of Elliott Wave and technical analysis tools is available in end-of-day or real-time versions using major data feeds.

Trend Reflection Trading System

www.trendreflection.com

Mechanical trading systems for TradeStation/SuperCharts cover 9 or 26 markets in diversified portfolios.

Trendsetter Software

www.trendsoft.com

Market analysis programs developed specifically for Mac computers include MacCharts, Personal Hotline, Personal Analyst, and Professional Analyst, powered by DBC's Signal data feed.

Trident Trading Systems Ltd.

www.trident-trading.com

Ticks and Tactics daily newsletter reports trading opportunities based on proprietary methods as well as methods from Gann and Elliott. Stock Index Array uses proprietary methods to determine minor and major points of support and resistance in stock indexes on an intraday time frame.

Ultra Trading Analytics Inc.

www.ultra-options.com

Ultra System is a set of applications and tools to support professional options traders via Internet or company intranet. Tools include Option Strategy Screening and Ranking (OSCAR), Calculation Worksheet position simulator, and Option Quote Chains.

Ward Systems Group (NeuroShell Trader)

www.neuroshell.com

This neural network software specifically designed to predict financial markets features 700 technical indicators and builds complex indicators and trading strategies with wizards instead of programming.

CHAPTER 3

Handling Your Order—
The Brokerage Connection

It seems a bit ironic, but one of the main reasons many traders give for moving into electronic trading is to get rid of their broker, the person who may have introduced them to futures in the first place and taught them about trading—or at least how to place orders. Right behind the brokers on the traders' hit lists are probably the floor traders, the less visible force blamed for every type of trading misfortune.

It's not that brokers and floor traders are so evil—for the most part anyway—but they represent bottlenecks for those who see the traditional futures trading process as an inefficient system operating at their expense. "They" are always out to get you, it seems.

What may be more irritating to traders is that they can't do much about it. They can change their data sources and their trading systems to help them make trading decisions. They can even change brokers. But they can't trade without a broker, the conduit for transmitting orders and taking care of the various administrative and fiduciary responsibilities that preserve the integrity of the market.

When the Commodity Futures Trading Commission approved negotiated commission rates for futures in 1978, it opened the door for the development of discount brokerage firms. In the 1970s, Merrill Lynch, Shearson, ContiCommodities, and other big firms dominated the futures trading scene and pretty much controlled the ability to accumulate and analyze data and information. Then new financial futures and options products came along, the introduction of the personal computer began to bring data analysis to the masses, and discount brokers started to flourish by offering reduced commission rates. Large brokerage firms decided to focus on the institutional marketplace and virtually abandoned the individual retail futures trader rather than deal with the hassles associated with numerous smaller accounts.

As discount brokers accounted for a growing share of futures trading, the business continued to be as competitive as ever as brokers tried to find an edge with lower rates. Today, the Internet has opened up new ways to increase efficiencies and reduce the cost of trading, but it could also be a threat to the future of brokerage firms and exchanges as they currently exist.

Of course, traders still cannot trade without an entity to handle their orders, and they can't trade without some kind of a marketplace where they can find a counterparty for their order. You either go with what the system offers you or you don't go at all. Neither the order-handling nor the trade-matching functions will ever go away, but the appeal of electronic trading is that both will become much more efficient in the future.

Traders have already made a great deal of headway in bringing this promise to reality. Before the Internet came on the scene, individual traders did not have access to much of the information that was available to institutions or large professional traders. Now individual traders can get real-time quotes, look at real-time charts, and evaluate real-time news and comments as quickly as the most sophisticated traders and can do so at a relatively low cost. Advances in technology and the ability of the Internet to distribute information to a wide audience is one step in the transformation to electronic trading. Many companies are already taking advantage of the Internet as a distribution channel, as indicated in the previous section. Brokerage firms are among them, using the Internet to disseminate their newsletters and other information, open accounts, send account statements, and so forth.

A second step in the electronic trading process really took hold in 1999 as brokerage firms rushed into online order entry. The list of firms in this chapter that offer online order entry is testament to the appeal of the concept. No broker wants to be without that capability. Imagine being able to streamline the traditional drawn-out process...

- Pick up a telephone. Oops, check to see if the brokerage firm is open first.
- Dial.

- Exchange pleasantries with the broker.
- Give your account number.
- State your order.
- Clarify your order.
- Hear your order repeated back to you.
- Give your okay.
- Hang up.
- Wait… and wait… and sometimes wait some more.

That's just to enter your order, and it usually doesn't take too long. Although you have already decided where you want to be in the market, based on the order you placed, you don't know where you actually are until you get a fill report. While you are waiting on the traditional trading process to let you know your position…

- The broker calls the trading desk or trading floor.
- A clerk answers the phone, hopefully on the first ring.
- The broker relays your order to the clerk.
- The clerk writes it out and hands it to a runner.
- The runner finds the firm's floor trader in the pit.
- The floor trader works diligently to execute your order.
- When filled, the floor trader confirms the order to the runner.
- The runner goes back to the clerk.
- The clerk calls the broker, when there is time to do so.
- The broker calls you with the fill.

Elapsed time? Who knows, from one order to the next?

That has been the all-too-familiar pattern in many markets. Orders that go straight to the floor, flash fills, and other steps have improved the process, but in fast-market conditions… well, not many things are more aggravating to an active trader than not having a fill and the brokerage firm not seeming as worried about it as you are.

Today's electronic traders can monitor real-time quotes and charts. When an opportunity pops up, they can click to their brokers' online order-entry page, type in an order in seconds (or it could already be "parked," waiting for a "submit" signal), send it directly to the exchange and in some markets, get a fill in a few more seconds. That's when everything is working smoothly on both your end and their end. That's what brokerage firms—and traders—expect to see consistently as electronic trading expands.

However, some of the hype about trading futures electronically has gotten a little ahead of reality and exceeds what firms can actually deliver. In some cases, online order entry is simply an alternative to the telephone for placing orders, and the trade desk continues to serve as a relay station on the order's way to the trading floor. Just as firms need to have an Internet site because everyone else does, firms also believe they need to offer online trading to keep up with their competitors. It is a marketing tool that capitalizes on what is possible in only a few markets so far. No matter how well brokerage firms perform their role in the trading process, they are limited by what is available at the exchange level.

Because day trading and online trading in stocks have been promoted heavily, many assume or have been led to believe that you can trade futures with your personal computer the way you trade stocks. That time is coming, but some aspects of futures make it more difficult for them to make the transition to the screen than it is for stocks. For one thing, the leverage factor that makes futures so attractive to traders can also be a huge liability. In today's volatile markets, the possibility of dangerous exposure for traders, brokerage firms, and exchanges can be opened up within moments. Until technology becomes more stable, controlling risks associated with futures will remain a much bigger challenge than it is in stocks, and the movement into electronic trading in futures will proceed more cautiously.

In the meantime, as brokers are making progress toward an electronic trading environment, many may find that mixing new technology with "old ways" of trading will continue to work better. Brokers and traders alike can agree that the Internet's ability to distribute large amounts of data and information to a large audience quickly is a major advance for electronic futures trading. Why mail newsletters or send out faxes when you have the Internet to disseminate trading recommendations, research reports, account statements, and other broker communications?

And brokers and traders alike can agree that the ability to enter orders online is a convenient facility for both parties when the trader has some experience. But it may not be the best channel in a business where customer turnover is one of the biggest concerns.

Conventional futures trading gives brokers a chance to know their customers and to help them understand how futures markets operate and what various orders can accomplish. In the push to the more hands-off style of online trading, a high-tech, high-touch approach may be even more important, according to Bill Kaiser, president of ZAP Futures in Chicago, which does 80 percent of its business electronically. "A lot of people are just getting used to the Internet, and a lot of people are new at trading. That's a lethal combination," notes Kaiser, who adds that it applies to new companies as well as new investors.

Brokerage firms do have many ways they can help you at several levels of commission rates. You may be a candidate for what the firms call "full-service," "broker-assisted," or even "discretionary" accounts. Even if you call a broker with your orders, you can get into electronic trading by getting online newsletters, recommendations, and market information for your pretrade analysis as well as current account statements.

This book targets the self-directed trader, that independent person who takes advantage of online resources to make a trading decision and places orders electronically without assistance. The critical question for you is, "Are you ready to be that kind of electronic trader?"

If you are an experienced trader who understands all the types of orders and what happens when you use them, placing your order online is rather simple and straightforward. You just follow the same steps you use with a telephone order. If your online order is completely out of line or you have made a mistake that exceeds the margin amount you have available, the broker's system is smart enough to reject it. That's the easy catch.

The difficult one is when your order is in line with reality, you have the margin money and you click "buy" instead of "sell," you forget to change the symbol from SP (full-size S&P 500 Index contract) to ES (E-mini S&P), or you give some other instruction that produces a result you don't want. Mistakes with online order entry are very easy to make because everything is moving so fast—and there is no broker to catch them. It doesn't take many mistakes to wipe out an account before you realize what you have done.

Some firms offer two levels of order routing, one direct to the floor and the other through the trading desk. Some customers request a quick check by a trading desk to give them—and the firm—a little comfort that a mistake has not been made in their order. Risk management software now makes margin checks so quickly that there is little delay in relaying orders to the floor. To go directly to the floor, firms may require customers to sign a separate document acknowledging financial responsibility and confirming that they are aware of how their orders are being handled.

Brokerage firms tend to be quite careful about monitoring accounts and, in some cases, make the decision for customers by not letting them enter orders online for more complex trades such as spreads or options, because these types of trades can be more confusing. Until you know your market and your orders, you probably should enter your orders through a broker, who can help you if necessary. That's what he or she is paid to do. That doesn't mean you have to take their trading recommendations, but the broker may catch a mistake and keep you out of trouble.

Besides, sometimes it's just faster or more convenient to pick up the phone and call in an order than it is to break away from your chart, get an Internet connection, find the online order-entry page, get a current quote... And, of course, not everyone can be in front of a computer screen or on the Internet all the time, so online order entry may not be an alternative in some situations.

The ultimate goal of the brokerage firm is to expedite your order as quickly as it can and to get you the best fill it can. To accomplish that, firms are using the Internet to transmit orders in several different ways:

1. Many link into the Trade Order Processing System (TOPS), a joint order-management product developed by the Chicago Mercantile Exchange (CME) and Chicago Board of Trade that takes orders directly to the floors of the major exchanges and sends order confirmation and fill information back to the trader in

a secure environment. TOPS printers are next to most pits.

2. Many link into CME Universal Broker Stations (CUBSII), electronic units that not only receive orders on a screen right in the pit but organize the order "deck" for the floor broker.

3. Many link directly into the CME's Globex system for immediate electronic order matching without using a floor broker in specific markets.

4. Some firms have developed their own electronic order-handling systems to take orders directly to their personnel on the floor. They do not want to put their orders into TOPS or some other system; they believe that causes them to lose control of the order. Instead, they prefer that the customer and the firm retain control over their own orders throughout the trading process by keeping them within their own system.

5. Some use the Internet primarily as a convenient means for transmitting orders from the customer to the firm, with the firm's trade desk relaying orders to exchange floors much as they have done in the past.

How a firm handles its online trading business often depends on its affiliation with another firm. An introducing broker (IB) may put its own spin on its online presence, but the services provided by its clearing firm are usually noticeable in what the IB offers. One prominent online system, for example, is LeoWeb, developed by Linnco Futures Group LLC (LFG). A number of affiliated firms (ZAP Futures, Futures Online, TradeCenter, and Futures Discount Group, to name a few) utilize LeoWeb's connection to the TOPS order-routing system and offer the LFG package of services to their customers.

E. D. & F. Man International Inc., which accounted for about 40 percent of the traffic flow through TOPS in mid-1999, is the clearing firm for its Jack Carl division and a number of IBs that offer Man's services. One of them, Ira Epstein & Co. Futures, has tailored its own online trading services to its customer base.

Other leading sources of online trading systems, either at their own firm or through their network of IBs, include Alaron

Trading Corp., Auditrack, BEST Direct (Peregrine Financial Group), First American Discount Corp., Interactive Brokers (Timber Hill Group), Lind-Waldock & Co., Refco, Rosenthal Collins Group, and Vision LP.

ONLINE SCREENS

What can traders expect to see on their screens with today's online order-entry systems? As you might expect, not all of the companies' screens look the same, but they have many similarities. Here, in general, is a summary of what you can expect to see on an electronic trading site.

Main Order Entry Page

Just like when you telephone your broker, this page covers the essentials of an order and is usually designed to expedite the entry process. In some systems you have to type in the contract symbol, price, etc.; in others, the chores have been trimmed to mostly point-and-click choices.

- Buy or Sell (or B or S radio buttons).
- Quantity (you can set a default or type in a number).
- Contract month and year (usually a click or two).
- Market (type in or pick from a menu you have customized for the most likely choices).
- A price for many types of orders (in some systems this is about the only test of your typing skills).
- Type of order (some label this column "modifier"; typically, you can pick from a list of popular orders, such as stop, limit, etc.).
- Duration of order (click on whether the order is good for today only, both day and night sessions, or until cancelled).

Options orders also require a strike price and a put or call choice, and spread orders require a few more keystrokes, assuming your broker allows you to enter those types of orders online.

Several additional comments about orders need to be interjected here. First, for most markets, the price you enter is rather simple. You enter prices the same way you hear or see them quoted, but usually without decimal points. Not everyone treats zeroes and decimal places the same way, and you will need to check the quoting service or brokerage firm to find out what their style is.

In the case of grains and soybeans, prices often include fractions—$2.32¾, for example. Most quote services and electronic trading systems, however, do not accept fractions, so most have adopted the system used by TOPS, which uses single digits to represent fractions. Some contracts are priced in fourths of a cent: 1 signifies ¼, 2 is ½, and 3 is ¾. So a price of $2.32¾ shows up on your screen as 2323. Options and MidAm contracts use eighths of a cent: 2 signifies ¼, 4 is ½, and 6 is ¾, making a $2.32¾ price appear as 2326 on your screen.

T-bond futures are priced in 32ds. Because fractions cannot be used, a price of 116³⁄₃₂ commonly becomes 116-03 when written, or 11603 on quote screens.

Experienced traders have become accustomed to these conventions, but newcomers may be a little confused about how to enter a price if they are facing an order-entry screen without the help of a broker.

A second note about orders involves the time of day you enter the order. Some firms have a blackout period following the close of trading, during which no orders are accepted for a specified period of time. You may intend for an order to be executed the next day, but if you place it during that period, it may never reach its destination, meaning an order you assume is placed may not be "working."

In the case of the E-mini or other contracts that have "night sessions" or extended trading hours, your order needs to make clear the period for which it is active. Most orders are considered to be for regular trading hours (RTH) or the "day session." The E-mini trades continuously from 3:30 p.m. until 3:15 p.m. the next day (Chicago time—CST). Your broker may hold orders entered after 3:15 p.m. until the day order desk opens in the morning, after which time such orders are worked until they expire. If it is after RTH and you want your order to be worked immediately, you should indicate as much on your order-entry form or phone your order to a night order desk.

A third note about orders is that just because your order-entry screen gives you a menu of orders from which to choose, not all types of orders are accepted by all exchanges or electronic trading systems. You will have to check with your broker to clarify what orders you can use.

When you have filled in all of the required boxes on your order-entry screen, you click on "create order" or "preview order" or a similar button that indicates you are ready to enter a trade. If you aren't quite sure about the order yet or you are waiting for the right circumstances, you may want to send the order to a "parked orders" or "pending orders" page to be ready for a trade later. For example, you might prepare a stop order and "park" it until you submit your main order so that when your main order is filled, your preplanned stop is ready to place immediately.

Preview Order Page

Here is your chance for a final review of the order before it is actually submitted. It is like the broker reading back your order to you to make sure it is what you want before you hit "submit order" or "transmit order" or "enter order." Or it may be a chance to think about the order again and edit it or scratch it. For example, a preview page often contains the last real-time price quote. In a fast-moving market, prices can change enough to negate the order you have set up or cause you to rethink what you want to do.

Confirmation Page or Working Orders Page

As soon as you hit "submit order," your order is on the way to the exchange. You will receive a confirmation—with an order number on it—that your order was received. In some systems all working orders must have two identification numbers, one from the brokerage firm and the other from TOPS, indicating it is a valid order. You can also click on the "working orders" button to reach the screen that shows you what orders are waiting to be executed and the current price of the market you are trading. A "refresh" or "update" button keeps you in touch with the status of your order and the current price.

Cancel or Cancel-Replace

Provided your order has not been executed, you can highlight it on your working orders screen and cancel it at any time or cancel and replace the original order with a followup order. If you are moving a trailing stop, for example, you can use cancel-replace orders to ride a market trend up or down as often as you want in an electronic trading situation, whereas you would probably exasperate a live broker if you tried to change stops with every price swing. In traditional trading, brokers often limit the number of cancel-replace orders they will take at no charge, but being able to issue unlimited cancel-replace orders is one benefit of electronic trading.

Fill Report

If your order is executed, you will receive an alert, or you can go to a "check fills," "today's fills and cancellations," "account activity," or similar page to find a list of the session's filled trades and dead trades and the price at which your trade was actually executed. As experienced traders know, that execution price can be somewhat removed from the current price or where you thought the fill should have taken place, depending on market conditions.

If you are trading one of the active electronic markets, this fill report should come back to you within seconds after you submit the order. In some pits, you may get a "flash fill" or some other quick notification of what your position is. In other markets where orders have to be executed in an open-outcry forum, however, it may take some time to get your fill, especially in volatile, high-volume situations, and if you are a small trader. One of the most frustrating experiences for traders is not knowing where their orders were filled or with some types of orders, even whether their orders were filled. This is particularly true for short-term traders, whose exact entry position is often the key to their next action.

Electronic order entry has helped brokerage firms get orders into the pit in a timely manner, but getting fills back out of the pit and reported back to the trader in markets other than those matched electronically remains too slow for the electronic trader in many cases. The perception is that brokers—and exchanges—in their anxiety to get the order, have not been as concerned about the mechanics of getting the results back to traders. Yet, if anything is providing the impetus to electronic trading, it is the promise of prompt fills.

Account Status

Wherever your trade was executed, you can see the results of that trade reflected on a "current positions" or "open positions" page if you are entering the market, or on a page summarizing the day's transactions if you closed a position. You can also access an "account status" or "portfolio summary" page, at which all of your positions are marked to market, giving you the total value of your account up to that moment. It also shows you the amount of margin required for your open positions and the amount of money you have left available as margin. You can click "refresh" or "update" or a similar button to get new values for all of these numbers with the latest tick from your price feed.

Account Statement

This electronic page is the same daily statement your broker receives and that you may receive in printed form in the mail a few days later. It summarizes your end-of-day situation.

Quote Pages

While you are trying to determine your order, you can refer to a customizable quote page that you have set up to include a list of the contracts you most want to see. Some brokers provide unlimited live quotes; others have a limit on the number of free page or quote views you can have. In either case, hitting the "view quotes" or similar page gives you a fast update on the futures and options contracts you have selected, including the last real-time price and such other information as net change, previous close, open, high, low, bid, ask, volume, open interest, and the time the exchange transmitted the price. You can also click on a "quick quote" or "get quote" button to get similar information for an individual contract if you are working on an order, are on a chart, or type in a contract symbol for the market you want.

KEY QUESTIONS

Assuming your broker does offer online order entry and you are comfortable with entering all the information on orders yourself, you still need to find out a few things about the firm beyond the usual questions about its financial soundness, the quotes/news/charts and other services it provides, and so forth. Those are important factors in opening any kind of account at any brokerage firm, but several other questions are especially relevant if you want to trade electronically.

1. Ask your broker where your order goes when you submit it. Despite claims of "direct to the floor" trading, some firms send your order to an order desk first, where it has to be checked and then reentered and relayed to the trading floor. In other words, you have gained a little by replacing the phone call to your broker with an online entry straight to the trading desk, and you can do this in the middle of the night if you like. But, your order can still get hung up on a trading desk and can be delayed before it is forwarded in a busy, volatile market.

Ideally, you should have signed the account form that allows your order to go directly to the exchange trade-matching system (for some contracts; see the chapter on exchange) or directly to the broker on the trading floor. If it is routed through the broker for risk-management purposes, it should make the briefest of stops in a computer before going to the exchange. As an electronic trader, you do not want to give up your speed advantage to the potential of having your order sitting on a trading desk.

2. Another question you might want to ask your broker is whether the online trading system is browser-based or whether you have to download software. *Browser-based* means that as long as you have a Web browser (generally Internet Explorer or Netscape) and a connection to the Internet, you only have to enter the URL (uniform resource locator) address your broker gives you, your user name, and your password and the trading screen appears on your computer. There is no software to download and no system to set up. It works on any computer with Internet access. Moreover, you can trade from almost anywhere that has an Internet connection.

A case can be made for either approach. It probably is not that big an issue to most traders, but it may be something you'll want to know if you get a little queasy any time you hear the words "download" or "upgrade." It's not a good idea to say it's easy or it's simple when it comes to any aspect of technology, but brokerage firms really have made the downloading process something you don't have to fear.

3.   A third question you will probably have for your broker involves the commission structure. Actually, that's the place most traders begin, and electronic trading has opened up a whole new discussion about lower commission rates. You may see rates from $4 per contract to $30 per contract and various sliding rates for volume. Obviously, you need to be careful about come-on rates like "trade for only $3 per contract" in large type and "for the first three trades" or "limited types of trades" in small type. Also, watch for any special fees that may be tacked on, including any additional charge for phone orders if you can't get through online, and whether the advertised rate is "per side" or "half turn" instead of round-turn commissions (a trade in and a trade out).

Technology reduces the costs of trading dramatically, and competition is driving rates to rock-bottom levels, making online futures trading attractive to active traders who trade a sizable number of contracts. Unfortunately for brokers, until some other arrangement comes along, commissions are how most of them get paid, and they have to go where the commission dollars are. Cheap commissions may force them to provide fewer services so they can handle more volume. Eventually, perhaps, brokers will be rewarded for training or mentoring or advising traders rather than solely on the basis of the number of trades (and commissions) they can generate, but until that happens, you will have to decide how much service you need and the amount of commission you will pay to get it.

One additional note: Check the results you get; you don't want to see what you saved with a great commission rate chewed up by slippage losses from trading errors and poor trade execution services. Poor fills can quickly offset cheap commissions.

Commissions can be a very important expense for an active trader, and they do need to be considered in any trading plan.

Important as they are, however, we have not included any rates in our listing of online brokerage firms (1) because commissions can change quickly and (2) because brokerage firms have so many ways to calculate rates for a specific trader that it is difficult to produce a comparison that is fair to all firms.

4.   A fourth question you can ask your broker may be the most important of all for the electronic trader, but it is the least likely to get a straight answer because circumstances change from market to market and from day to day. The question is, "How reliable is your service?"

Technology being what it is, there still are times when software problems or exchange problems or something else can take an online system down. The small print in most account agreements informs you that the brokerage firm does not assume liability for your positions in those situations. Neither do the exchanges. In other words, if you have a large S&P position and the market is moving and the broker's online system goes down just as you are trying to get out of the position, you are not absolved of responsibility for that position. Brokerage firms say they will do everything they can to help you trade, but ultimately, you are still the one at risk.

Although the risk of system failure should decline as technology continues to advance, this is a big issue for the electronic trader in futures, where even a few minutes' lapse can result in large price swings producing huge losses. It may not happen very often, but you should find out from your broker what happens when a system fails and what kind of backup plan your broker has.

FINAL EVALUATION

Evaluating a brokerage firm for your electronic trading comes down to three things:

- Performance: How well does it really handle your orders and execute your trades?
- Package: What services are provided to help you make a trading decision?
- Price: Does it provide the best value, the best tradeoff between what you pay and what you get?

The broker checklist (in Table 3–1) will guide you through some of the factors that are important for electronic trading. Selecting an online broker isn't as easy as filling out this simple checklist, of course. You may have a few straight yes or no answers, but you probably will add a lot of notes to many of the answers. For example, on charts, do you get the front month only or all months? Or on flash fills, a firm may have that capability in one pit but not in another. If you can get flash fills in financial markets but not in cattle and you trade cattle, you probably will want to note that.

In addition, a "yes" checkmark does not indicate whether the service provided will be sufficient. How good are the quotes or charts or research reports for your purposes? How good are the fills and how fast are the fill reports? You can ask your broker the questions, but many answers will be subjective, based on your own experience.

This checklist just provides electronic traders with some topics they might like to check out at a firm's Web site or discuss with a broker. Also keep in mind that you are aiming at a moving target, since firms are constantly adjusting their services and improving their products.

In the end, despite all the electronic interfaces and the enthusiasm about online trading eliminating the people that stand between you and your trade, the selection of a broker who can handle your electronic trading desires usually comes down to one thing, the human element. How are you treated? Do you have confidence in the people with whom you are dealing?

Order execution and other aspects of electronic trading may become more like impersonal commodities themselves, with little differentiation among firms, but it is likely to be the people who still make the difference when you decide where to trade.

We can't speak to the people factor, but the next section lists brokerage firms that indicate they have online trading capabilities in futures. Many new players jumped into online trading in 1999, so the number of firms is growing, and this list undoubtedly is not complete. Some firms are introducing brokers (IBs) of larger clearing firms, and you may want to check the clearing firm's listing for more information on the type of online trading services the IB offers.

TABLE 3—1

The Electronic Trader's Online Broker Checklist

Feature	Yes	No
Browser-based system		
Download system software		
Real-time price quotes		
Quote page can be edited		
Quotes available by telephone, pager, or other quick means away from PC		
Real-time charts		
Delayed/end-of-day charts		
Are charts programmable? (add trendlines, technical studies, etc.)		
Real-time news headlines		
Real-time news stories		
Daily market commentary		
Company research reports online		
Access to outside research		
Calendars, key report facts, contract specifications, etc., online		
Real-time account status		
Access to daily account statement		
Create orders mostly from menus		
Order details filled in automatically by clicking on contract symbol or chart		
Current quote on order screen		
Parking orders possible		
Preview of actual orders		
Cancel-replace orders page		
Options, spread orders accepted		
		(Continued)

(Concluded)

Feature	Yes	No
Orders go direct to floor (no stopping at trade desk for review)		
Orders go directly into electronic exchange (e.g., E-mini into Globex)		
Working orders status page		
Account activity page showing day's trades		
Fill alerts		
Flash fills		
Broker assistance available		
System trading for customers available		
Overnight trading available		
Backup trading plan		
24-hour "emergency" support		
T-bill policy		
Fill In Numbers for Items Below		
Minimum account size (overnight)		
Minimum account size (day trade)		
Commission rate for online trading		
Commission rate for telephone trade		
Commission rate for broker-assisted trading		
Special offers		
Special features not covered above		

One other important note: We have not attempted to rate any of the firms. If you are interested in ratings, you can check an Internet site such as SmartMoney (**www.smartmoney.com**), the joint Dow Jones/Hearst Corp. site, which reports on studies conducted by Gomez Advisors, Piper Jaffray, and others. This research tends to focus only on equities, including online and discount services. Another useful site directed primarily to stocks is

Online Brokers Guide (**www.investforlife.com**), which offers the Online Trading Tips newsletter edited by Liam Naden.

If you want anecdotal comments from traders about their experiences with various futures brokerage firms, Donald Johnson of Santa Rosa, CA, (**www.sonic.net/donaldj/futures.html**) and Mark Brown of Texas (**www.markbrown.com**) are among those who maintain Web pages for this purpose. Keep in mind that their comments may be somewhat dated, tend to lean toward the negative side, and may not reflect most traders' current experiences.

ONLINE FUTURES BROKERAGE FIRMS

Some firms that offer online order entry have Web sites that can be accessed only by customers who enter their user name and password. Other firms require registration to get free information, which means you are probably a "lead" and are likely to get a phone call soliciting your account. So a Web site listing here may not mean you will be able to get information about the firm online.

For more information about an introducing broker's online services, because of their connection to the clearing firm, you can go to the listing for the clearing firm indicated to see what might be offered. We have checked every Web site listed and believe information given about the firm is correct, but in trying to condense the contents of a Web site into a few lines, we have necessarily had to generalize and may have omitted some things, or the firm may have added or discontinued features in the interim. Inclusion on this list does not suggest or imply any endorsement or recommendation for any firm, nor does the lack of a listing suggest anything negative about a specific firm.

Abbreviations used often in this list:

CBOT—Chicago Board of Trade
CME—Chicago Mercantile Exchange
TOPS—Trade Order Processing System
CUBS—CME Universal Broker Station
IB—Introducing broker
FCM—Futures commission merchant

CTA—Commodity trading advisor

S&P—Standard & Poor's, usually used in connection with S&P 500 Index contracts

ABG Investment Group

www.abgdirect.com

This guaranteed IB to E. D. & F. Man International Inc. features i-Net Direct! browser-based order entry using Auditrack technology. Live demo accounts are available during the day.

Access-Direct Discount Trading

www.access-direct.com

This is a Cedar Rapids, IA-based IB.

ADM Investor Services

www.admis.com

ADMIS serves as an FCM clearing partner for more than 150 IBs and 600 associated persons around the world. Market research materials disseminated through IBs include daily comments, biweekly and monthly newsletters, in-depth reports on special market conditions, and Conrad Leslie's Daily Market Letter.

Advantages in Options

www.optioncaddie.com

"Passport" registration is required for access to this free site, which specializes in high-probability, low-frequency, volatility-based trades, including options "insurance" strategies.

Alaron Trading Corp.

www.alaron.com

Alaron has one of the cleanest, snappiest Internet sites (see Figure 3–1), offering Alaronline as either a browser-based program that requires no software download or as Windows-based trading soft-

FIGURE 3–1

Sample Screen from Alaron

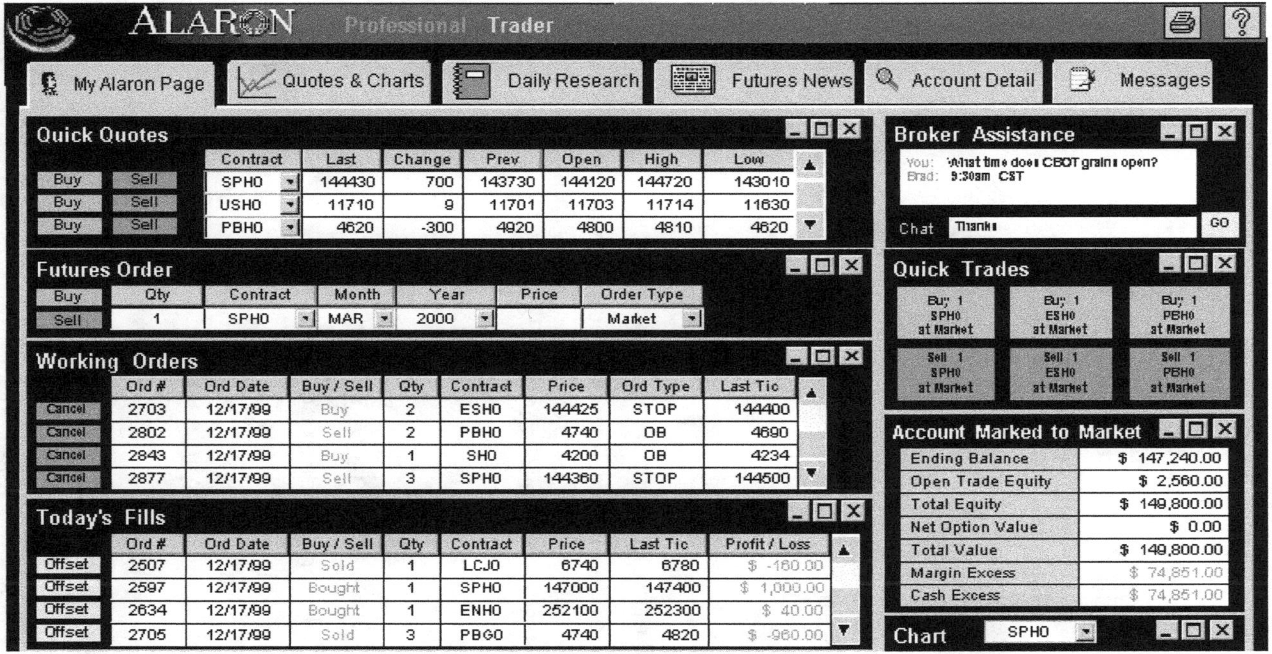

Alaron has most of the important information you need on one screen. In addition to the order form, you can see current quotes, working orders, today's fills, open positions, news headlines, a current chart, and your account status all at a glance. Moreover, there is a section for one-click quick trades and a chat room.

ware you can download. Part of Alaron's educational philosophy is to provide quotes, news and research reports at no charge without requiring that you be a customer. Using services powered by FutureSource, you click on quotes and then a market to get 10-minute delayed quotes for all contracts for that market. You then click on a contract symbol to get a chart for that contract. Charts can be modified for several time frames (15 minutes to monthly) in several different styles with several different studies. The news feature from Futures World News/Bridge lists the headlines, and a click takes you to the full-text version of the story. You can also use keyword search. All of the firm's latest market research is online, including 11 free proprietary daily research reports from company analysts and special situation reports. If a U.S. Department of Agriculture crop report is released in the morning, Alaron's analyst puts an interpretation online soon after the report, or you can get e-mail updates if you are a customer.

Allendale Inc.

www.allendale-inc.com

Allendale's fee-based services include a premium package of unlimited quotes and Futures World News comments, Traders Market Center software to analyze data, and the Allendale Advisory Report with advanced charts, a 14-page agricultural report updated four times daily and available via the Internet.

Alpha One Trading (A1T)

www.alphaonetrading.com

This Costa Mesa, CA, IB to Alaron Trading Corp. trades all markets online and offers a paper trading account. Registration is required to receive quotes and charts with analytical studies.

Altavest Worldwide Trading Inc.

www.altavest.com

Altavest is a San Juan Capistrano, CA, IB to LFG LLC. It offers direct access to trading floors via LeoWeb, live market commentary in the TradeScope newsletter, and proprietary research as well as the iTrade real-time charts and quotes package.

American Futures & Options

www.afutures.com

This Naples, FL, IB to Vision LP offers Internet Order Express online trading, delayed quotes from Vision or Findbrokers, trade recommendations, and interpretations of technical indicators by JAH Research and Trading.

Angus Jackson

www.angusjackson.com

This Fort Lauderdale, FL, IB's customer accounts are maintained and cleared at E. D. & F. Man International Inc. Orders are placed through TOPS or phoned directly to the trading floor with no intermediary trading desk.

Arrow Futures & Options

www.arrowfutures.com

A guaranteed IB of LFG LLC in Chicago, Arrow uses the LeoWeb electronic trading system. Arrow offers research, charts, and delayed quotes as well as access to live audio in the S&P and bond pits for a monthly fee.

Auditrack

www.auditrack.com

This simulated brokerage service based in Boca Raton, FL, can be used as a learning tool by a beginner or as a way for experienced traders to test out a new trading strategy in actual market conditions without risking actual money. The Internet system used to trade Auditrack accounts is Auditrade, which is used by some brokerage firms as their Internet system for real online trading.

Beddows Commodities Inc.

www.bcifutures.com

BCI Futures is a full-service IB in Florida offering execution and clearing services and 24-hour worldwide trading capabilities.

BEST Direct

(See Peregrine Financial Group.)

Buffalo Trading Group Inc.

www.buffalo.pair.com

Paul McKnight's Arlington, VA, IB focuses on scale trading, also called interval-based trading. The Web site includes links to a number of scale trading resources.

Cannon Trading Co. Inc.

www.e-futures.com

Cannon is a Beverly Hills, CA, IB of LFG LLC, that uses LeoWeb to transmit orders directly from customer PCs to the trading pit. Cannon also offers iTrade, LFG's Internet-based quote and charting program, Market Voice, and LFG research.

Capitol Commodity Services Inc.

www.ccstrade.com

This Indianapolis, IN, IB's site includes an education center with free articles or links to articles on trading as well as quotes, charts, research, and more for registered users.

Chicago Futures

www.chicagofutures.com

This division of Chicago FCM Kottke Associates LLC offers direct access to electronically traded markets and quotes and charts powered by FutureSource.

Chicago Futures Investment Group (Futureswatch)

www.futureswatch.com

Amoabin Futures Co., a Chicago IB, offers this fully integrated online order-entry service with online market quotes, news, and research, plus futures trading and training sessions for day trading and overnight trading.

Cleartrade Commodities

Clearwater Commodities

www.cleartrade.com

An IB for E. D. & F. Man, these divisions of S. R. Joss Inc. have offices in Chicago and Clearwater Beach, FL, and offer free daily trade recommendations via e-mail.

Columbia Asset Management

www.usafutures.com

As a Portland, OR, IB of Vision LP, Columbia offers Internet Order Express Millennium (IOXM) electronic trading, Vision's Automated Client Information System (VACIS), Sim-U-Trade, and an extensive Web site that includes information on managed futures investments and various CTA programs. IOXM interfaces with Internet Order Express Wireless, which enables you to trade in your car, from pool or beachside, or virtually anywhere you want. VACIS is a 24-hour center of futures information accessible via touchtone phone.

Commodity Futures and Options Service

www.cfos100.com

CFOS is an independent IB based in Houston and offers LeoWeb electronic trading and access to a number of CTAs with managed account services. Charts are provided by TFC Commodity Charts.

Commodity Resource Corp.

www.commodity.com

This Incline Village, NV, firm clears through Refco. Online services include George Kleinman's Market Alert, weekly advice and trade of the month commentary, quotes and charts from the exchanges, and Tradesignals.com.

Compass Financial

www.compassfinancial.com

Compass is a Richardson, TX, IB offering a number of services online, including links, calendars, contract specifications, streaming or delayed quotes, etc. Many pages are free but password protected, requiring users to register.

Crown Futures Corp.

www.scaletrading.com

A full-service firm based in Fairfield, IA, Crown specializes in the scale trading approach. Services include the Crown Commodity Investment Letter and daily market commentary written by owner Hal Masover.

Currency Management Corp.

www.forex-cmc.co.uk

Established in 1989, CMC is a London-based foreign exchange market maker and futures brokerage firm. CMC was the first firm to offer clients real-time Internet dealing in foreign exchange (in May 1996) and has since become the biggest Internet forex trading company in the world, handling around 50,000 transactions each month on its Market Maker V4 software, which is also used by some major banks. The Internet dealing service is not routed via the World Wide Web but is a live direct connection between dealer and client. Normal deal execution time is two seconds. CMC is an execution-only institution that does not manage client funds nor trade its own account. Clients make all of their own trading decisions; CMC views its role as getting clients the best dealing prices possible and giving them market intelligence and news to help them make decisions. CMC does not pay commissions or parts of the dealing spreads to third parties, such as introducing brokers or sales people, but deals directly with clients in more than 55 countries. About half of CMC's customers are from the U.S.

CyBerCorp.com

www.cybercorp.com

Formed in 1995 in Austin, TX, CyBerCorp is an electronic trading technology group that develops high-end, real-time electronic trading and execution systems for day traders and active investors. CyBerBroker Inc. provides online brokerage services and trading technology on the Internet, specifically CyBerTrader and CyBerX. It also operates as a service bureau to third-party broker-dealer clients who utilize CyBerCenter's server, network, and brokerage infrastructure and support operations. CyBerTrader is used by more than half of the U.S. day trading rooms. The company started by building trading software for high-volume day traders and then expanded the business to the Internet. When CyBerBroker accepts an order, CyBerX immediately directs it to whichever electronic network or market maker is offering the best price at that moment. The Windows-based application includes real-time streaming quotes with unique graphical displays.

Dallas Commodity Co. Inc.

www.dallascommodity.com

Dallas Commodity is affiliated with Rosenthal Collins Group LP (RCG), using the RCG Direct Internet order-entry system to route orders, check current market conditions, and review account and order status. The Web site's trading tools section includes free quotes, charts, calendars, weather maps, and links to many sources.

DH Financial LLC

www.dhfinancial.com

DH Financial is a Chicago-based FCM offering the Global Trade Execution (GTEX) electronic trading system as well as software analysis products as a solution development partner with IBM. GTEX is an independent, proprietary system that maintains control over orders (see Figure 3–2). Depending on the expertise of the trader, orders can be routed directly to the trading pit where handheld computers help traders execute trades, or they can go through the firm's trading desk, where they can be reviewed for both the customer's and the firm's protection and then forwarded to the pit. Direct orders to the floors complete the trade process in about 15 seconds under normal market conditions. GTEX also has a module that allows customers to paper trade in real-time with real prices so they can learn about a market or test a new trading system in actual market conditions without the monetary risk. DH's software products include Cycle Trader, based on the theory of cycle analysis coupled with multiple indicators and oscillators. DH also offers an educational program for online trading and market commentary if you register.

Discount Futures Brokerage

www.discountfuturesbroker.com

An IB of ADM Investor Services Inc., Discount Futures Brokerage places itself between the full-service broker and discount broker. Customers receive *The Lingle Strength & Weakness Indicator for Domestic Futures*, President Rob Lingle's proprietary publication, by fax, mail, or e-mail.

ECommodities

www.e-contracts.com

ECommodities is a Dallas, TX, full-service brokerage affiliated with Coquest Inc., an independent IB and CTA, and offers direct online order entry via LeoWeb and electronic trading tools (charts, quotes, news, weather) included in iTrade.

FIGURE 3–2

Sample Screen from GTEX

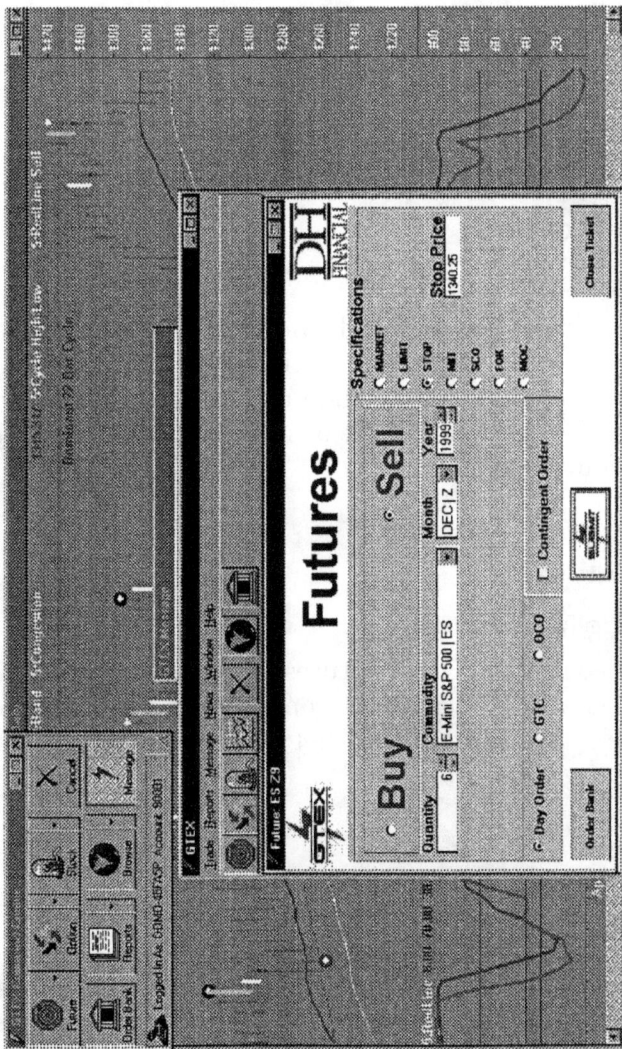

Everything is point-and-click; there is no typing on the DH Financial order-entry screen, which makes buy and sell choices very clear and provides icon links to key pages.

efutures.com

www.efutures.com

This is the online trading division of Futures Express, a Platteville, WI, IB. It uses electronic trading and order-routing systems such as Globex, TOPS, Electronic Clerk, and CUBS 2 and flash fills when electronic order entry is not an option. The Web site offers live news, delayed quotes, and charts powered by FutureSource.

The Eiger Group

www.eigerfutures.com

The Eiger Group, based in Ridgefield, CT, consists of three corporations, including Eiger International Inc., an IB of E. D. & F. Man. Web site offerings include day trading and daily trading recommendations and a table of trend indicators, with some information in German.

Excel Futures

www.excelfutures.com

Established in 1998, Excel Futures is based in Huntington Beach, CA, and is affiliated with Alaron Trading Corp. It offers individual investors 24-hour Internet trading services and managed account programs.

Excel Systems

www.exlsystems.com

Excel Systems is a division of LFG LLC that specializes in the design and execution of proprietary futures trading systems. The entire trading operation is built around system trading, with systems custom-fit to clients who specify their risk parameters, the markets they wish to trade, and whether to day trade or position trade.

Excel Trading Group

www.xltrading.com

This is a division of LFG LLC providing services for its IBs and foreign brokers. Excel offers the various LFG order-entry, research, and other services, including 24-hour placement of orders through the Internet (including the overnight markets).

Farr Financial Inc.

www.farrfinancial.com

Farr Financial is an independent, full-service brokerage firm in Santa Clara, CA, offering the PMBe online order-entry platform to customers. Orders can be placed through a professional trade desk or electronically to PMBe handheld devices in the pit or directly into electronic exchanges for all U.S. and European futures. Online services include the Vardon Report and technical analysis market commentary.

Field Financial Group

www.fieldfinancial.com

Field Financial, located in McLean, VA, is a guaranteed IB for First American Discount Corp. It uses a browser-based system for online order-entry and account information. Online tools include links to exchange price quotes, or customers can get real-time quotes via INFOline 24 hours a day.

First American Discount Corp.

www.fadc.com

First American, based in the Sears Tower in Chicago, has an active online business support system for IBs based on Auditrade technology. It offers customers of these firms a browser-based online trading system that lets them place orders, receive confirmations, and check account status, all at the click of a mouse button, with no additional hardware or software other than basic Internet access. Free services online include 15-minute delayed quotes from North American Quotations Inc. for all U.S. futures exchanges. A personal quote monitor lets you store up to 10 quotes on the markets of your choice. FirstCharts provides daily charts on more than 40 markets, with the ability to apply up to five different technical indicators. Market commentary is provided by a number of brokers with their own home pages. Simulated brokerage service is available in connection with Auditrack to learn how to trade or test strategies. Links to affiliated vendors offer other services or products at special rates to First American customers.

Fox Investments

www.foxinvestments.com

Fox is a division of Rosenthal Collins Group LLC in Chicago and offers the Fox Global electronic trading system for online trading. Fox Global features an opening screen with a number of file-folder tabs that take you to pages to enter orders, monitor market prices, check account status, etc. Free online quotes and charts are powered by FutureSource: click on a menu of markets to go to a quote page, then click on a contract symbol to get a chart for that contract. Fox also offers market commentary and access to several advisory services as well as Trade Tutor, a software program to train people how to trade.

Freeman & Co.

www.betterfutures.com

This Valley View, CA, IB describes itself as a "boutique outlet" clearing through LFG LLC and using LFG's LeoWeb service for online trading direct to the pits. An associated CTA, Toni Financial, specializes in short-term trading strategies trying to capture modest profits consistently. It provides a daily advisory service free to brokerage customers or for a fee to noncustomers.

Futech Commodity Services

www.futechcommodities.com

Futech is a Moorhead, MN, IB clearing through LFG LLC and using LeoWeb for order entry. Its Web site offers links to INO's

Quotewatch and exchange quotes and charts, weather sources, news, LFG research, and other LFG services.

Futures Direct

www.futuresdirect.com

Futures Direct is the direct-to-the-floor business of Saul Stone & Co., an FCM with offices in Chicago and New York that has been clearing trades for more than 75 years.

Futures Discount Group

www.futuresdiscountgroup.com

This Chicago firm clears through LFG and offers an online trading service called ROCKET that can be downloaded to a PC and gives customers direct connections to major exchanges and to the TOPS order-routing system.

FuturesOnline

www.futuresonline.com

FuturesOnline is a division of LFG. As its name implies, it focuses on online trading for futures and cash foreign exchange with 24-hour access to cash and exchange-for-physicals markets. A browser-based Internet trading platform allows customers to place orders directly to the floor in seconds, monitor positions in real-time, place orders direct to foreign exchange dealers, and more, in an encryption security system that protects the integrity of your account while you are online (see Figure 3–3). Futures and options spreads can have up to four different legs. Futures Online news and research features regularly scheduled daily, weekly, and quarterly reports. Trading tools include LFG's iTrade quote and charting package, Market Voice audio commentary, and other trader resources. FuturesOnline also sponsors "million dollar trading contests" in which the trader with the highest rate of return wins a $1,000,000 proprietary trading account at LFG. In addition to Internet brokerage services, FuturesOnline also offers broker-assisted trading through Daniels Trading Group, another division of LFG.

FIGURE 3-3

Sample Screen from Futures Online

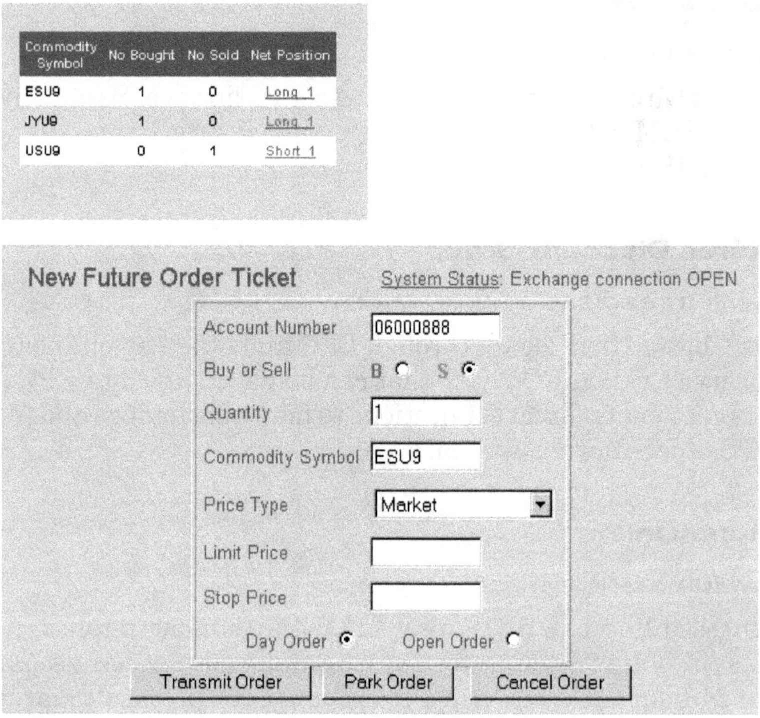

Commodity Symbol	No Bought	No Sold	Net Position
ESU9	1	0	Long 1
JYU9	1	0	Long 1
USU9	0	1	Short 1

New Future Order Ticket   System Status: Exchange connection OPEN

Account Number	06000888
Buy or Sell	B ○ S ◉
Quantity	1
Commodity Symbol	ESU9
Price Type	Market ▼
Limit Price	
Stop Price	
Day Order ◉	Open Order ○

[Transmit Order]   [Park Order]   [Cancel Order]

This FuturesOnline screen keeps track of all net positions, and a click of the mouse takes you to the basic order-entry screen that can get you out.

FuturesBusiness

www.online.futuresbusiness.com

This Atlanta IB's online and order-entry site is Alaronline from Alaron Trading Corp., and it provides customers with access to trading accounts and the ability to place orders, get real-time quotes, etc., online, 24 hours a day. Technical advice using Advanced Get and TradeStation software is available to full-service customers.

FutureWise Trading Group

www.futurewisetrading.com

FutureWise is a Northville, MI, IB for Vision LP, offering Internet Order Express, Sim-U-Trade, and other Vision services for Internet or full-service trading.

Global Forex Trading Ltd.

www.gftltd.com

This foreign exchange dealer specializes in trading services for individual and corporate accounts wishing to speculate and hedge in the interbank foreign exchange market. Clients get instant access to spot currency markets through the online order-entry system, WebForex, and real-time data and charting through the Global FX Data Center. GFT offers clients dealer quotes that are 5 pips wide on major markets and also operates a 24-hour dealing desk to service clients worldwide.

Hi-Tech Futures Inc.

www.hi-techfutures.com

Hi-Tech Futures, an IB in Tampa, FL, clears through Alaron Trading Corp. and transmits orders over the Internet directly to the floors of the major commodity exchanges without going through the TOPS system or any other trading terminal. The Trading Command Center offers Alaron news and research pages and charts from TFC Commodity Charts.

Infinity Brokerage Services

www.infinitybrokerage.com

This Chicago IB clears all trades through LFG LLC. Infinity Direct is the name of the firm's LeoWeb software program, which allows customers to enter and track their trading activities using their personal computers. The software can be downloaded from Infinity's Internet site. Registered users can try a 30-day test account with access to charts, quotes, research, options software, and more.

Interactive Brokers LLC

www.interactivebrokers.com

Interactive Brokers is a member of Timber Hill Group that provides online execution services in listed equity and equity-based derivatives in the United States and Europe. That includes the equity index futures contracts traded at the London International Financial Futures Exchange, Eurex, Globex, MATIF and MONEP in Paris, and the Hong Kong Futures Exchange. Depending on the product, customers are connected directly with a specialist book, a trading pit, or an electronic exchange. Equity and index options, futures, and options on futures are routed electronically directly to traditional open-outcry trading pits to an executing broker who holds a wireless handheld computer, or in the case of fully automated exchanges, directly to the order book. Resellers who route customer orders through Interactive Brokers include a number of major brokerage firms. The Interactive Trader Workstation (see Figure 3–4) offers customers error-free transmittal of order information; speed in placing, modifying and cancelling orders; and speed in confirming executed trades. Trader Workstation software runs on Windows 95 and Windows NT platforms.

Iowa Grain Co.

www.iowagrain.com

Iowa Grain is a full clearing member of the Chicago futures exchanges specializing in the U.S. agricultural futures and options markets. The OAK online Internet order-entry system does not provide graphics, analysis software, news feeds, or features from quote vendors but concentrates only on moving orders from customer PCs to the trading floor as quickly as possible and whenever possible, directly into pit broker terminals for immediate response. The browser-based architecture of OAK features the floor-order ticket form interface and is integrated with back-office systems to allow real-time position and account views. Every order is automatically screened electronically in a fraction of a

FIGURE 3–4

Sample Screen from Interactive Brokers

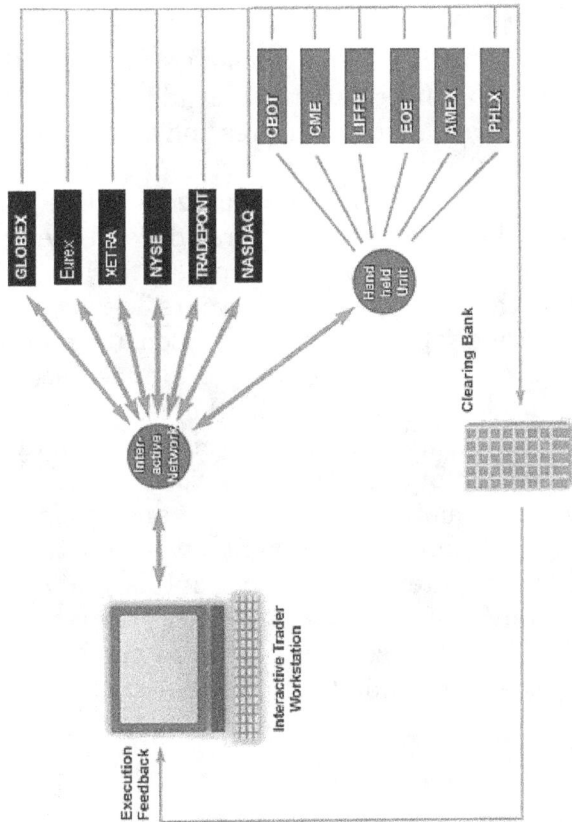

After you point-and-click to enter your order on an Interactive Trader Workstation, it is routed electronically by Interactive Brokers to an exchange, where it is received by either an electronic system (top group of exchanges) or on an Interactive Broker handheld computer in the pit. You can modify, cancel, or cancel-replace your order until the point of execution. Confirmation of a trade is routed back to your Interactive Trader Workstation instantly.

second when it is entered. In addition to daily market comments and access to more than 250 research reports, special features of Iowa Grain include a virtual crop tour that goes directly into the fields using the latest digital camera technology, and Internet Audio Advisor, audio market comments on demand.

Ira Epstein & Co. Futures

www.iepstein.com

Focusing on serving the individual trader, this Chicago IB clears through E. D. & F. Man International Inc. and features IraTrade Internet trading for fast, efficient futures and options order placement along with up-to-the-minute market information and analysis (see Figure 3–5). IraTrade is available in online HTML or stand-alone, downloadable software versions, and the firm suggests traders have both for backup purposes. "We have not had both go down at the same time in 1½ years," reports company president Ira Epstein. The company has automatic margining, a process that sets the appropriate margin for each account and speeds orders through a quick check and directly to the trading floor. Ira Epstein offers a wide range of services, including Commodity-Fone for touchtone telephones, a voice-activated system that can deliver live quotes 24 hours a day and report fills. You can also get fax-on-demand quotes, eight advisory hotlines, opening market calls, computerized callbacks of fills, and account information online. The firm also provides Irachart charting software, OptiVal Iraoption software, intraday audio pit commentaries, analyst comments and recommendations, and teaching videos.

Jack Carl Futures

www.jackcarl.com

A Chicago division of E. D. & F. Man International Inc. that has been in the discount brokerage business since 1983, Jack Carl offers Man's complete execution and clearing services, with 24-hour worldwide trading capabilities and a range of support services to help people trade independently. Online trading is available through Jack Carl's Electronic Trading Center

FIGURE 3-5

Sample Screen from Ira Epstein & Co. Futures

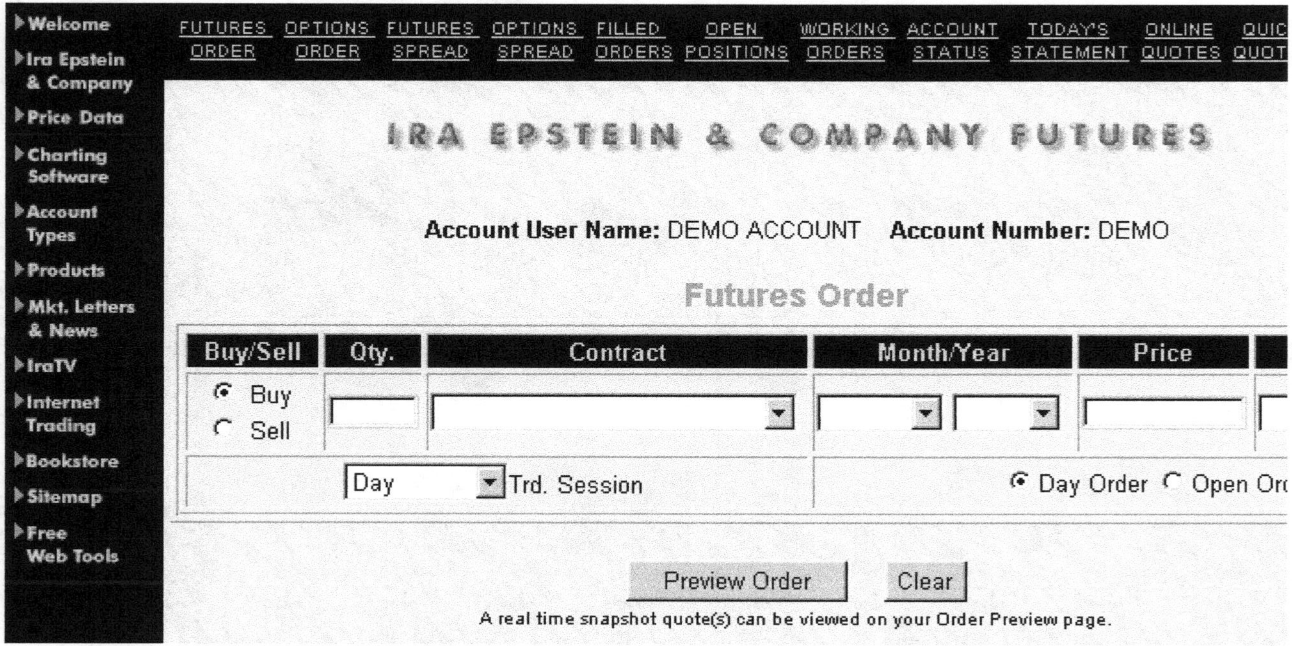

Buttons on top of this Ira Epstein & Co. futures order screen let you select your choice of order. Links on the left side take you to a wide range of resources offered by the firm.

(**www.jcetc.com**). You can place trades 24 hours a day, including spread and options orders (see Figure 3–6). The customer toolkit area provides direct access to selected trading tools that assist customers in making trading decisions. The Trader's Resource Center includes real-time quotes and news in association with Data Broadcasting Corporation, charts from Market Research Inc., news headlines and movers from CBS MarketWatch, a commodity calendar recreated from *Futures* magazine, and contract and margin information from exchanges.

Jones Ag Marketing

www.jonesagmarketing.com

Jones is an IB with ADM Investors Services. Located in Mahomet, IL, it emphasizes trading in grain futures and options. Jones does not sell newsletters or products but focuses on executing trades. A browser-based Internet order-entry system allows 24-hour trading in actual or in simulated accounts using Auditrack's Auditrade.com online brokerage system.

Keystone Discount Commodity Brokers

www.keystone-web.com

Keystone is a division of LFG LLC and has offices around the world. Customers can send orders directly to the floor from their PCs, using free software to access the server or using the Weborders system to place orders from the Web site. The Web site includes links to a number of resources as well as interesting comments on and links to sources for dozens of economic indicators.

Lakefront Futures & Options LLC

www.lakefrontfutures.com

Lakefront is a Chicago IB clearing through Iowa Grain Co. and offering online order entry through the OAK Trading System. Customers get real-time online access to their trading accounts and more than 250 free market research reports.

FIGURE 3-6

Sample Screen from Jack Carl Futures

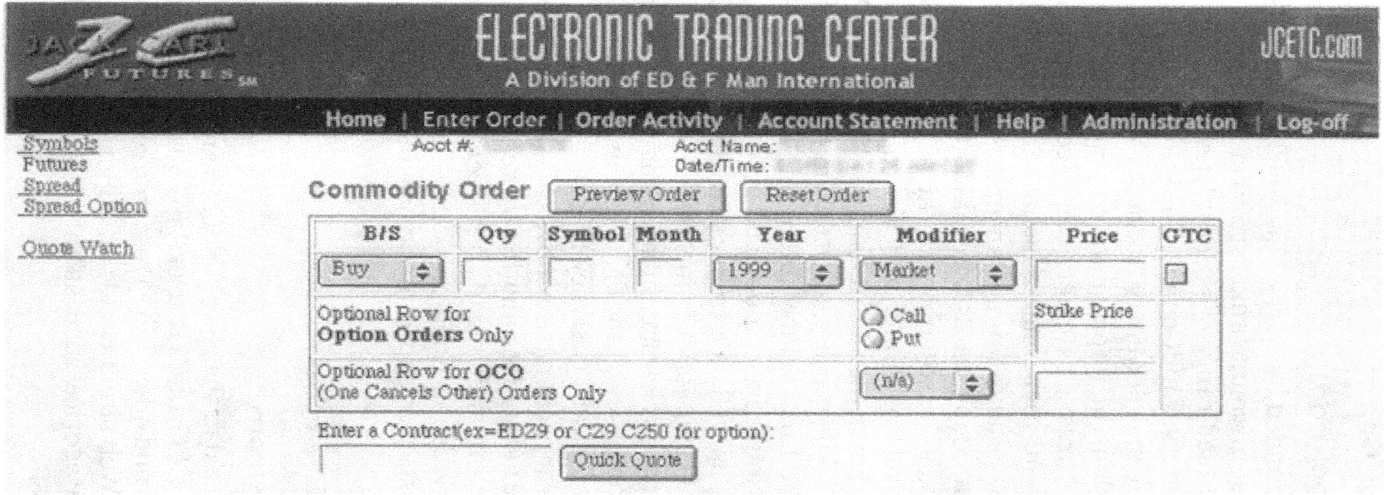

Jack Carl's Electronic Trading Center features three easy-to-use order-entry templates, enabling customers to place orders ranging from the simplest futures transaction to the most complex options spreads.

Lind-Waldock & Co.

www.lind-waldock.com

Lind-Waldock, founded by Barry Lind in Chicago in 1965, is the oldest and largest discount brokerage firm in the futures industry and offers a broad range of services, including full online capabilities for traders. LindConnect Online Trading (see Figure 3–7), a pacesetter in order-entry systems that has gone through several generations of improvements, includes a number of customizable features. Customers can access a personal quote page, with up to 40 real-time snapshot quotes, 500 times in a month at no charge and can get an up-to-the-last-tick view of their trade and account status by clicking the "refresh" button. Lind customers can also subscribe at a discount to eSignal Internet, delivered real-time, and get continuously updating market quotes, charts, news, fundamental data, etc. When you want to make a trade quickly, a button on the quote page takes you directly to the LindConnect order-entry page. Online trader tools include various levels of delayed quotes, charts, news and weather services as well as a trader's catalog offering books and other resources. Other services include Lind P.R.O.F.I.T., which provides simulated brokerage for learning or experimenting in actual trading conditions; LindFX, a dealer in global foreign exchange spot and forward currency transactions, including cash-to-futures trades or exchange-for-physicals (EFPs); LindSystems, which trades your system or another system for you; and a wide variety of account arrangements. Trade centers in Chicago, New York, London, and Hong Kong provide 24-hour service using an order express system to expedite the handling of orders.

Link Futures

www.linkfutures.com

Link Futures, based in the New York Mercantile Exchange building, is an IB for LFG LLC. It uses LFG's LeoWeb electronic order-entry system and offers LFG's research commentary and other services. Link's Web site includes an ambitious listing of dozens of sources in categories such as intraday quotes, after-hours

FIGURE 3–7

Sample Screen from Lind-Waldock & Co.

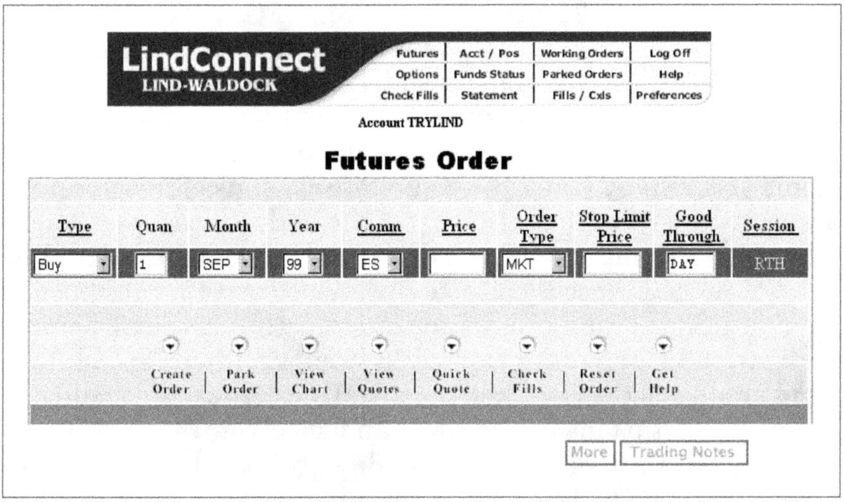

The LindConnect futures order page from Lind-Waldock & Co. is typical of the many things you can do with an online order-entry system. "Create order" gives you a chance to preview your order before you submit it. "Park order" lets you put an order aside to submit later, a handy feature if you are waiting for an order to fill and want a stop ready to go when it does. "View chart" gives you a chart, and "Quick quote" gives you the last quote for the market on the order screen. "View quotes" takes you to a page that you customize to get the current quote and other details on up to 40 contracts. "Check fills" takes you to a page that gives you the details of a fill, if any exist. Several "lightning bolts" in the upper right corner of your screen alert you when you do have a fill. The tabs on top of the screen let you check up on your "working orders," "parked orders," "fills and cancels," and various current account status pages. A chance to set "preferences" or get "help" is also just a click away. And, of course, you want to be sure to "log off" when you are done trading if there is any chance someone else might have access to your computer. If you do not log off, soneone could also have access to your account.

quotes, intraday charts, daily charts, commodity commentaries, and so forth, cross-referenced by market so you can get the sources of all types that apply, for example, to bonds, or you can just get all the sources in one category, such as *news* (more than 20 links).

Linnco Futures Group (LFG LLC)

www.lfgllc.com

Headquartered in Chicago's Sears Tower, LFG is one of only a few FCMs that are full clearing members on all U.S. futures exchanges. It has become one of the leaders of the electronic trading movement, offering a full range of order-entry facilities, from central and special services desks to floor desks, to arb desks, and electronic order entry. The LFG Web Suite consists of five different applications, which are also part of the online trading packages offered by a number of IBs on this list that clear through LFG. LeoWeb is the Linnco Electronic Order-entry system, designed to eliminate phone calls and written orders by linking customers directly to the TOPS order-routing system, a joint order-management product of the CME and the CBOT. Orders are also routed to CUBS workstations at the CME and Electronic Clerks at the CBOT. E-mini orders from TOPS go directly into Globex. Fill information is transmitted back to the customer's PC through the LeoWeb system. A companion to LeoWeb is the Account Information Manager (AIM) module, which allows users to download up-to-date account information directly from the LFG server. AIM eliminates the need for e-mailing, faxing, or mailing account information, adding greater efficiency and more security to trading. iTrade provides real-time quotes and market information, including LFG market research reports. Traders can customize the data into a format of their choosing. MarketVoice brings the latest information from the floor of the exchange to the customer's desktop, with more than 50 scheduled live audio broadcasts supplemented by news to give customers the feel of what is happening on the trading floor. INFOLine is useful for traders who are always on the go, providing real-time market information updates from any touchtone phone. Quotes and account status can be accessed wherever and whenever customers want. LFG's information services department provides customized information to the retail broker, delivered via satellite, fax, bulletin board, or Internet.

E. D. & F. Man International Inc.

www.edfman.com

E. D. & F. Man, headquartered in London, has a 200-year involvement in international trading and a long history as one of the world's principal suppliers of sugar, cocoa, coffee, edible nuts, and spices to international branded food and beverage manufacturers, particularly in the confectionery and soft drink industries. In the1980s, Man extended the expertise it had gained in trading agricultural futures and hedging price risk to develop its brokerage business outside the agricultural markets. Since then, it has expanded to become one of the world's major futures and options brokerage firms, offering services to clearing firms and private clients. It is one of the most active firms today in expanding the electronic trading market, serving as the clearing firm for a number of IBs. In mid-1999, Man International had the largest TOPS network, accounting for about 40 percent of the traffic over TOPS.

Matrix Trading Group Inc.

www.matrixoptions.com

Matrix is a full-service guaranteed IB of First American Discount Corp., located in North Palm Beach, FL. Registration is required for most information on the Web site.

Meppen Trading LLC

www.meppentrading.com

This Chicago firm specializes in trade execution services.

Merchant Capital Inc.

www.merchantcapitalinc.com

Merchant provides brokerage facilities for individual, corporate, and institutional accounts globally and uses Merchant Direct, provided by LFG, for its online trading technology. The browser-based online order-entry system requires no software downloading. Order numbers come right from the trading floor and are not generated by a server that could leave orders in cyberspace somewhere. Password-enabled services include real-time, delayed, or end-of-day quotes or charts; LFG's research, Market Voice or Market Squawk; news sources, such as Futures World News and Hightower Report; and other resources.

MG Financial Group

www.forex-mg.com

Money Garden Financial Group is an Internet-based company dedicated to introducing the foreign exchange market to self-traders and enabling them to trade currencies online. The firm is one of the largest players in the retail forex market, serving both institutional and individual clients. It has been in business since 1992 and on the Internet since January 1997, opening up trading in the forex market from the big banks and $100,000-plus accounts to individuals with accounts as small as $1000. MG Financial Group focuses only on the spot currency market, allowing clients to trade four major currency pairs—euro/dollar, dollar/Swiss franc, dollar/Japanese yen, and UK sterling/dollar. Forex trading is not bound to any one trading floor but is done electronically among a network of banks continuously over a 24-hour period. Internet and phone trading can be done 24 hours a day, 5 days a week.

Net Discount Futures

www.netdf.com

This brokerage firm's online order-entry software sends orders directly from your PC to exchange floors. E-mini orders are routed directly to Globex for electronic matching, with fills reported on your screen in as little as 5 to 6 seconds. S&P orders are routed directly to the CME's CUBS station in the S&P pit.

NetFutures

www.netfutures.com

NetFutures in Chicago clears through LFG LLC and uses ROCKET as its Internet electronic order-entry and fill-reporting system. ROCKET's connection to the TOPS order-routing system takes orders created on a PC directly to the floors of the principal exchanges and reports fills back to the PC automatically.

Nihon Unicom Corp.

www.unicom.co.jp

This Japanese FCM offers its customers real-time quotes on Japanese futures markets, 16 kinds of technical charts for Japanese markets (daily and weekly), position detail sheets, market comments and bulletins on exchange rates, Nikkei averages, and major commodities.

Op Wiz Inc.

www.biznet.maximizer.com/opwizinc

Op Wiz is a guaranteed IB of Vision LP in Chicago and offers online trading via Vision's Internet Order Express along with other Vision services, such as daily and intraday trade recommendations and market commentary, Sim-U-Trade, etc. Quotes and charts come from FutureSource.

Orion Futures Group Inc.

www.orionfutures.com

Orion Futures Group, a Tampa, FL, IB, uses Vision LP as its clearing FCM and offers such Vision services as online trading with Internet Order Express Millennium, VACIS (Vision's Automated Client Information System for touchtone phone information), a free paper-trading program, and other market information.

Paragon Investments Inc.

www.paragoninvestments.com

Paragon is a guaranteed IB of Vision LP based in Rose Hill, KS. It offers Internet Order Express and other Vision services for self-directed traders placing orders on their own behalf. Paragon's free services to customers include FutureSource for quotes and charts, Jim Hyerczyk's Comprehensive Trading Service, news from several leading sources, weather from Intellicast, and other resources.

PAT Systems Ltd.

www.patsystems.com

PAT Systems, based in London, creates Personal Automated Trading Systems that offer a total software solution for brokers wishing to give customers direct access via a Windows PC to a growing number of electronic futures and securities markets throughout the world. The software enables customers to route orders directly to the broker's host system, which performs an instantaneous risk check against the originating account prior to forwarding the order to the relevant exchange for automatic execution. PAT Systems' PTS (Personal Trading System) also offers users access to a real-time charting and analytical service. PTS Real-Time Charting uses the PATS price feed to run SnapDragon, which offers the ability to display historical and intraday charts and also includes a whole range of technical studies and indicators. Traders accessing the system over an Internet dialup can have complete intraday charts even if they are not connected throughout the whole session.

Peacock Trading Inc.

www.peacocktrading.com

Peacock Trading, an IB in Oswego, IL, offers the latest in electronic trading technology in association with LFG LLC, using the LFG Web Suite to harness the power of technology via desktop. The Web site includes free futures lessons for beginners and answers questions new traders frequently ask.

Pearce Financial

www.pearcefinancial.com

Pearce Financial, Destin, FL, is a specialized brokerage for worldwide clients and an IB with R. J. O'Brien & Associates. It was the first R. J. O'Brien IB to integrate the R. J. O'Brien Client Access Terminal (RJOCAT) trading system into its order-entry process. RJOCAT connects directly to the TOPS network, including a direct link into Globex for E-mini trades, CUBS, and 20 printer locations on exchange trading floors in Chicago, New York, and

Kansas City. Pearce also has a simulator site for traders to get acquainted with the online trading systems.

Peregrine Financial Group Inc. (PFG)

www.flight2quality.com

BEST Direct Division

www.pfgbest.com

PFG is an expanding Chicago FCM offering online trading with its BEST Direct communication software, a stand-alone system utilizing Windows technology for speed and flexibility. (BEST is short for Bressert Electronic System Trading, designed by Jerome Bressert.) Automatic upgrades ensure that all customers have the most current version. BEST Direct (see Figure 3–8) accepts

FIGURE 3–8

Sample Screen from BEST Direct

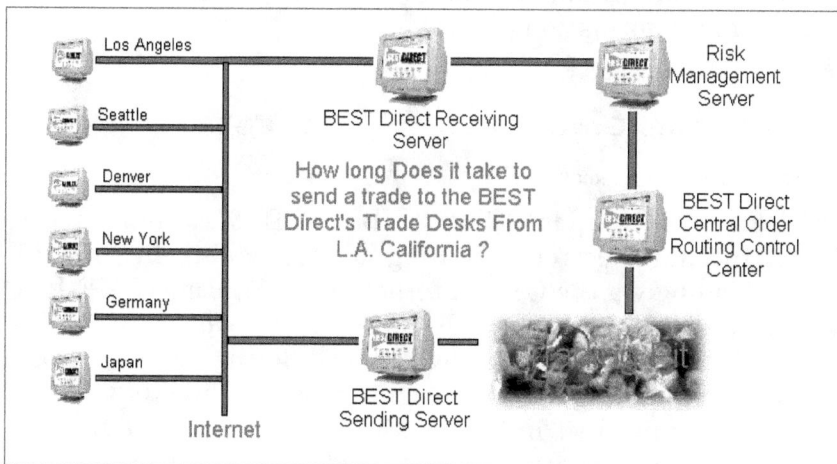

One of the most effective pages of the BEST Direct Order Management System demo page on the Internet uses an animated display to show how fast an order can get from Los Angeles (or Denver or Germany or anywhere) to the trading pit: 1 second, even though it goes through receiving, risk management, and routing centers. The system visually displays when an order reaches the trade desk by changing colors when it is received, filled, cancelled, or rejected.

all types of orders and indicates on your order-management screen the price at which the order has been placed and the current price, showing real-time open position status. The main system screen is color-coded for a quick visual analysis of your account activity, highlighting fills, cancels, working orders, parked orders, and other details. Instant messaging directly to the trade desks provides quick two-way communication without the normal Web e-mail delays. A key difference between BEST Direct and many other online services is that BEST Direct decided to bypass routing orders through the increasingly overloaded TOPS system and, instead, set up its own direct online order-entry system. A real-time risk management system checks orders in an instant and relays them to the trading floors with no delays. Other PFG resources include DayTRADER Pro, a day trading program; quotes and charts powered by FutureSource as well as exchange quotes or DBC Signal real-time quotes at a discount; weather, government reports, and other fundamental information; Walter Bressert's market-timing analysis; Floyd Upperman research; and the Futures Factors newsletter. Best Direct is also offering its TurnKey IB program to IBs to set them up with complete online trading and information programs.

Price Futures Group Inc.

www.pricegroup.com

Price Futures Group is a Chicago IB of E. D. & F. Man International Inc. Its Electronic Trading Division offers PriceCenter online trading via the CME Internet Order Routing (CME-IOR) system and the Interactive Broker trader's workstation. The CME-IOR, a browser-based Java applet offering basic electronic order entry and order management, connects directly to TOPS and provides a direct link through TOPS into Globex for electronically traded contracts. PriceCenter is designed to be an Internet futures trading portal to launch multiple online systems, access real-time account information, and find relevant trading reference information. Charts for registered customers are from Market Research Inc.

Prime Time Investment Services Inc.

www.primetimetrading.com

Prime Time is a Chicago IB clearing through Iowa Grain Co. and offering online order entry through the OAK Trading System.

Professional Market Brokerage (PMB)

www.pmbinc.com

PMB is a Chicago FCM for self-directed accounts and CTA, CPO, and IB execution services for all futures and options with brokers fluent in Arabic, French, German, Greek, and Italian. PMBe, the firm's online service, routes orders electronically through Interactive Brokers and the Timber Hill Group directly to handheld devices located in the trading pit for major markets at the CME, CBOT, and London International Financial Futures Exchange, and directly into the electronically traded markets at Globex and Eurex, reducing the transmission time for executing orders to a minimum. PMBe also has a system trading service for customers, using the fastest online execution. Among the news and information services offered by PMB is Advanced Technicals by Gil Vanderaa III.

Quant Trading Inc.

www.quant.com

Quant Trading Inc. was founded in 1989 to develop and market the Sector Trading System, a comprehensive trading system that merges electronic trading with trading desk analytics and straight-through processing. Customized stations within the Sector Trading System support the needs of traders, sales people, and risk managers.

Rand Financial Services Inc.

www.rand-usa.com

Rand Financial, a Chicago FCM, features Rand Online, which uses Theodore as the electronic order system to send orders, receive fills, manage working orders, and confirm daily activity. Its flexible open network architecture accommodates a wide range of configurations and communications options to support open-outcry trading. For example, if a client has only one account, the account number can be the default value on the order-entry screen. For clients with multiple accounts, the most frequently traded accounts can be user-programmed on the speed buttons on the screen so that the touch of a button brings up the appropriate account. Using proprietary software that Rand provides, the client's screen looks like a standard trade ticket. To place orders, clients can use a touchscreen, mouse, or keyboard to enter information. Hitting the green "send" button sends the order to the screen at Rand's booth on the trading floor within seconds (orders are not routed through TOPS). Market orders are hand-signaled to the floor trader. For limit orders, bar-coded order tickets are printed out and delivered to the floor trader. Clients can place orders on their screens and have them given to Rand's floor brokers in under five seconds. Fills on market orders are hand-signaled back to the booth and entered directly on the screen. Limit order tickets are returned to the booth where the bar code is scanned to bring the order to the screen and fill information is entered. Fill information is transmitted immediately to the client as well as Rand's broker group and back office, giving customers, brokers, and the firm virtually a real-time picture of positions. Because it is strictly an Internet system, clients can be connected live to Rand Online all day for the price of a local telephone call, a feature that especially benefits international clients. (The Web site is available in German and Japanese versions.) Rand's Client Data Services menu provides access to daily statements, with an account summary for the prior day's trading activity, mark-to-market reports showing open trades marked to the current price, daily trading activity files for today's trades, and personal archives of previous daily statements.

Refco Group Ltd.

www.refco.com

Refco Group provides a broad range of global financial services to institutional clients worldwide through its subsidiaries and affiliates. Services include the execution and clearing of futures and options on regulated exchanges and prime brokerage of interbank foreign exchange, U.S. Treasury securities, nonferrous metals, precious metals, nondollar securities and equities. Refco research includes daily and weekly reports on all markets, preopening and closing audio broadcasts, audio analysis of key U.S. and European economic releases, and crop reports, in-depth reports on markets, and Internet slide shows (5- to 10-minute slide and audio presentations on various markets). Access to the research Web site is available to Refco clients for a nominal monthly fee.

R. J. O'Brien & Associates Inc.

www.askrjo.com

This Chicago FCM provides clearing and back-office functions for affiliated brokerage firms in more than 30 states and offers online services through the R. J. O'Brien Client Access Terminal (RJOCAT) trading system based on Auditrack's technology. RJOCAT provides front-end access to the TOPS network, including a direct link into Globex for E-mini trades, Electronic Clerk at the CBOT, CUBS2 at the CME, and 20 printer locations on exchange trading floors in Chicago, New York, and Kansas City.

Robbins Trading Co.

www.robbinstrading.com

Robbins Trading is an IB of Robbins Futures Inc., an FCM in Chicago. In concert with the Professional Services Division of Rosenthal Collins Group, Robbins offers Robbins Online direct floor access to key markets. Its electronic order entry couples Internet access with direct-to-the-floor backup routing and 24-hour access to Globex, Project A, and foreign markets, allowing around-the-clock order entry. INFOline provides 24-hour dialup quotes, and foreign exchange desk trading is also available. In addition to other brokerage services, Robbins offers its System Assist trading program and sponsors the annual World Cup Championship of Futures Trading.

Rosenthal Collins Group LLC

www.rcgdirect.com

Professional Services Division

www.rcgpsd.com

Rosenthal Collins is an international full-service FCM based in Chicago. Its Professional Services Division, based in Los Angeles, provides customized/boutique services. The firm's electronic trading features ifutures with Swarm Technology, an advanced multiorder routing system that integrates six different systems—TOPS, CUBS II, Globex, Digital Turret Technology, Interactive Brokers' workstation, and the CBOT Electronic Clerk systems—into one centralized network, sending orders to the appropriate marketplace. ifutures is engineered to provide greater velocity, reduced slippage, and increased reliability to ensure seamless trading in turbulent market conditions. By giving customers direct control over order transmission, ifutures lets them decide when and where a trade is executed with no need to depend on anyone else to direct their orders. ifutures' key windows include the order tablet window that spells out the details of an order; the order management facility window that lists working orders, filled orders and other order status items; and the trading profile window that sets up all sorts of default conditions the way a typical "settings" or "preferences" page does. Rosenthal Collins provides a number of other FCM services, including direct pit access to qualified customers, client-specific execution, 24-hour interbank foreign exchange trading, managed accounts, and various information sources.

R.S. & Associates

www.euro4cast.com

This European commodity trading and research company uses the WebTrader software in combination with the Fibonacci Trader for real-time, multiple time frame charts and the Financial Market Navigator software and strategy. Its Web site offers real-time data, real-time charting, and analysis. In cooperation with its

Dutch partner and introducing broker, DIM Europe, orders can be placed with the trader workstation, which executes orders via the Internet on major world markets within seconds. Among the specialties of this firm is advising major airlines on price movements of jet fuel, foreign exchange, and interest rates.

Saddle River Futures Trading Group Inc.

www.saddleriverfutures.com

Saddle River Futures Trading Group in Chicago is a guaranteed IB of Refco Inc., offering the research resources and online trade execution services of Refco.

SMART Futures

www.smartfutures.net

SMART (Superior Market Access for Retail Traders) is a Chicago firm clearing through E. D. & F. Man and offering online trading with Trade Express, which takes orders direct from the customer to the trading pit. Order entry is by point-and-click or by typing in information. An account status screen shows mark-to-market updates on all daily cash balances and open positions. SMART uses LFG research, analysis, news, and other information services.

Spectrum Commodities

www.atthemarket.net

Spectrum is a guaranteed IB clearing through E. D. & F. Man International and offering its clients Man's execution services and access to world markets. Spectrum provides clients a customized service plan. Resources for clients include a monthly newsletter, *Perspectives*; the *Daily Technical Update*, a one-page review of support and resistance areas and technical comments on current market movements; and the *Trade Focus*, a "case study" perspective released 2 to 4 times a month as situations occur.

STA Trading Services

www.stafutures.com

STA Trading Services is a guaranteed IB located in Memphis, TN. In addition to brokerage services and the STA Trading Package containing commentary, trading recommendations, and other advisory services, STA offers Online Ag Marketing, which gives agricultural marketing and merchandising services for five crops.

Striker Securities Inc.

www.striker.com

Striker is an independent IB and a registered securities broker-dealer in Chicago, specializing in providing trading systems, trading advisor research, and other trading services to investors. The firm also offers trading system consulting as well as futures managed accounts by CTAs. Striker's PITLINE is a direct-access phone line service to process orders for the S&P 500 futures pit and the T-bond futures and options.

Super Fund Financial Group Inc.

www.futures-trading.com

This is a promotional Web site for products and services from Vision LP (see below).

Trade Center Inc.

www.tradecenterinc.com

Trade Center, based in Laguna Beach, CA, is an international brokerage service offering services ranging from individual trader guidance to global real-time Internet online order execution (see Figure 3–9). As an IB to LFG LLC, Trade Center offers LFG services, including LeoWeb electronic order entry, INFOLine 24-hour quotes and information, flash fills in sensitive markets such as S&P 500 Index and T-bond futures, proprietary LFG research, Market Voice floor reports and daily hotlines, 24-hour account and position information, and more. A nightly checkout fax ser-

FIGURE 3-9

Sample Screen from Trade Center, Inc.

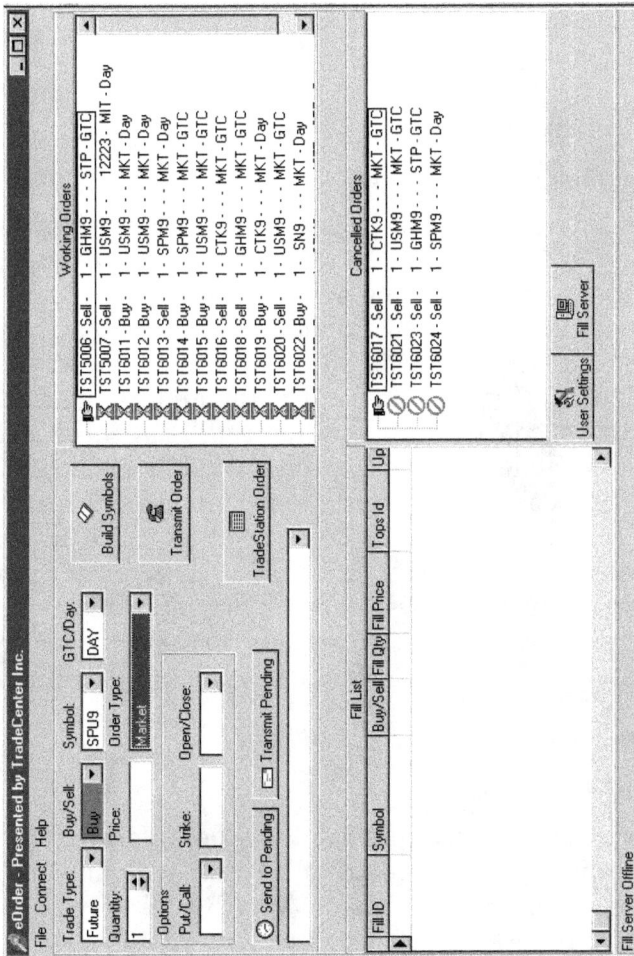

In addition to order information, this Trade Center page provides a complete list of working, cancelled, and filled orders and gives you a button for a TradeStation order, reflecting the firm's ties to Omega Research's analytical software products.

vice confirms all trades transacted during the day. Trade Center specializes in professional system monitoring and in assisting systematic traders. It emphasizes technical support and training seminars for TradeStation and other Omega Research products and makes available to customers its systems and indicators library. Parts of its Web site can be viewed in French, German, Italian, Portuguese, or Spanish.

Trader's Network Inc.

www.tradersnetwork.com

Trader's Network is an IB in Loveland, CO, clearing through R. J. O'Brien & Associates Inc. and offering R. J. O'Brien's services, including its online trading software, which Trader's Network calls Flash. If you click on a quote, you can send an order, get a chart, or access news stories on that contract. For a fee, Trader's Network offers Traders Market Center, an all-in-one package of quotes, news, charting, and online trading at three levels. Special offers include *A Trader's Handbook: The Reversal Day Phenomenon*, a book explaining the reversal day indicator based on market action/reaction, and Trade Simulator Pro, a paper trading program with 12 years of historical data on 22 commodities and 12 technical indicators, allowing you to click through a month of trading action in minutes to speed up the learning process.

VIP Futures

www.vipfutures.com

VIP Futures (the name represents Value, Information, and Performance) is a guaranteed IB of Rosenthal Collins Group LLC and is located in San Francisco. VIPDIRECT allows online traders to enter orders directly using the Internet and their PCs, bypassing the broker for faster access to the order desk where orders are routed to the most efficient marketplace. This multitasking platform means online traders are not locked into one system but receive a "ticket number" instantaneously, signaling the order is in the market. VIP offers 24-hour real-time quotes, 24-

hour global trading, 24-hour order placement, and the facilities to execute a trade within seconds at any exchange in the world.

Vision LP

www.visionlp.com

This New York FCM is one of the larger providers of introducing brokerage services in the U.S., with more than 130 IBs representing approximately 500 registered associates and an estimated 50,000 futures trading customers over the last few years. With the move into online trading, Vision offers Internet Order Express Millennium (IOXM) and Vision's Automated Client Information System (VACIS) to a number of traders via its extensive network of IBs. IOXM is a complete browser-based electronic order-entry system sending orders directly to CUBS terminals at the CME and the CBOT's electronic system. It provides customizable pages of live quotes and easy tracking of orders, including more complicated option and spread orders that other systems do not accept. IOXM interfaces with Internet Order Express Wireless, which enables you to trade in your car, from pool or beachside, or virtually anywhere you can imagine. VACIS, described as an "android broker," provides futures information via any touchtone phone 7 days a week, 24 hours a day. Sim-U-Trade is a simulated brokerage service that lets you learn how to trade on paper in real market conditions without risking real money.

World Link Futures Inc.

www.worldlinkfutures.com

World Link is an IB in Huntington Beach, CA, offering a trading course for beginners and a real live paper-trading account before you open an actual account. Special services include the Trader's Forecast, a survey of trader opinion about a particular topic, with compiled results released to survey respondents Monday morning, and a cattle and livestock section established for livestock industry people that contains information on using futures and options to protect livestock business profits. Charts on the Web site are powered by TradingCharts.com Inc.

Xpresstrade LLC

www.xpresstrade.com

Xpresstrade is a Chicago guaranteed IB affiliated with ADM Investor Services. It provides self-directed futures traders with high-speed Internet trading services, market data, trading tools, and up-to-the-minute account information. The Xpresstrade system supports a wide variety of futures and options order types and is the first Internet-based futures broker to offer a totally electronic contingent order capability, allowing you to enter primary and contingent orders simultaneously without any assistance from a human broker: "If my original order is filled, then I'd like this protective stop order and/or this limit order at my profit target to be entered automatically." Contingent orders may be entered either at an exact price or at a specified distance from the price at which the original order is executed. An interactive charts program uses Java programming language to create personalized charts of all major U.S. futures contracts. Long-term futures charts are provided by FutureSource/Bridge; real-time news comes from Futures World News/Bridge.

ZAP Futures

www.zapfutures.com

ZAP Futures is a division of LFG LLC, the Chicago futures FCM that clears all U.S. futures exchanges. The ZAP 2000 electronic trading system (see Figure 3–10) is a multifunction platform that has connections to the TOPS order-routing system, taking orders created on a PC directly to the exchange trading floors. In addition to the LFG services, the ZAP Total Trading Platform interfaces with various quote and information vendors providing real-time quotes, charts, and other important data. If you are watching the S&P market on a Signal quote screen, click on the ZAP button and a ZAP order screen pops up. If you have a trading system on analytic software such as TradeStation, signals can be transferred automatically into orders so you can set up your plan in the morning and come back in the afternoon to see what trades it made. A simulated trading program is available. Interactive futures charts are provided in association with

FIGURE 3–10

Sample Screen from ZAP Futures

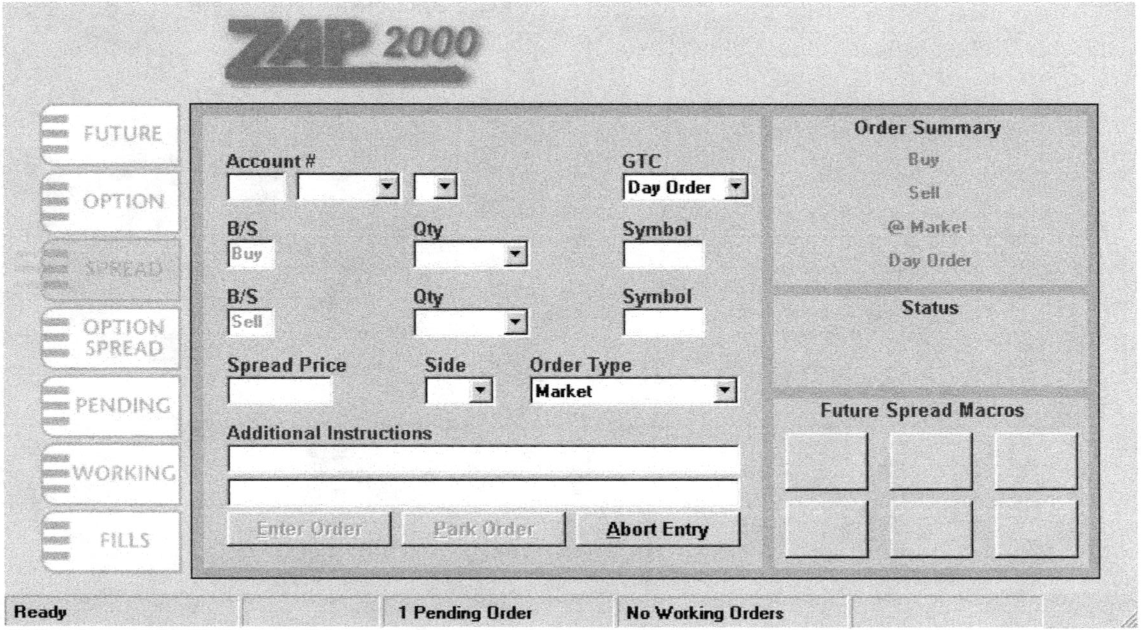

This futures spread order page on the ZAP Futures 2000 electronic trading system allows traders to make spread macros and gives them a place for additional instructions to the broker if they have a specific plan in mind for their order.

Tradesignals.com. A unique feature is that with every trade, traders can earn "ZAP dollars," which can be redeemed for merchandise or discounts on service packages such as ZAP Audio, an Internet-based "squawk box" service.

CHAPTER 4

Executing Your Trade–
The Exchange Function

With all the data and information available today on the Internet and with online order entry now feasible, it might seem like the electronic trader is all set for the future. But no matter how well today's software and information services analyze markets and no matter how well brokerage firms expedite customer orders, today's electronic futures trader runs into limits at a most crucial point, the exchanges where trades must be executed. Only a few U.S. markets currently offer true electronic trading, and they have a few restrictions and limitations that keep a throttle on electronic trading activity.

It's not as if the U.S. exchanges aren't taking some steps to get to the electronic future, but some of the biggest advances in electronic trading have come from overseas, while U.S. exchanges have been embroiled in political squabbles, centering primarily around the interests of their membership. Nearly all of the futures exchanges outside of the United States already are or are going electronic. One of them, Eurex, formed by the merger of the Deutsche Terminborse (DTB) and the Swiss Options and Financial Futures Exchange (SOFFEX) in 1998, has surpassed the Chicago Board of Trade (CBOT) to become the world's leading exchange for futures and options trading volume. Dramatic increases in 1999 propelled the electronically traded German bund contract at Eurex into the No. 1 spot among futures contracts traded around the world, exceeding the CBOT's open-outcry T-bond contract, the longtime leader.

BACKGROUND

When a group of traders branded as the "Young Turks" began to play a prominent role as leaders in the U.S. futures industry in the late 1960s, current prices were posted on chalkboards at the exchanges. In a bow to new technology, Polaroid camera photos of the chalkboard were used for the official time and sales reports at one point. The first electronic price boards were installed when the Chicago Mercantile Exchange (CME) moved into new facilities in 1971.

Then the young leaders expanded the vision of trading with new contracts in totally new areas. Following futures on the meats in the 1960s came futures on the ultimate commodity, money, as currency futures began trading at the CME in 1972 and interest rate futures at both Chicago exchanges in the mid-1970s. The CBOT's spinoff of the Chicago Board Options Exchange (CBOE) in 1973 launched a new marketplace with a new trading instrument. Futures contracts on gold, energy, and stock indexes and then options on futures and stock index options joined the scene by the early 1980s as exchanges engaged in a competitive race to develop new products to expand their business. By the mid-1980s, exchanges and brokers had plenty of new products to offer; they just needed a way to trade them more efficiently and for longer hours.

The early solution for handling more volume in more markets was to add more people, more pits, and more space. But it became clear that trading floors could accommodate only so many bodies as exchanges tried to balance the demand for more pit space with brokerage firm demand for more booth space. Futures commission merchants (FCMs) faced similar growing staff and space problems trying to build up their order desks and offices to handle more business in more markets. As technology developed in the 1980s, the firms migrated to the computer for their back-office accounting and record-keeping functions, but they still needed front-office solutions to handle the flow of increasing orders.

To facilitate the trading process, the CME and CBOT worked together to develop the first generation of the Trade Order Processing System (TOPS) to handle order flow more smoothly. The goal of TOPS was pretty simple: Move people off the floor to order desks upstairs and give them electronic connections to the floor. You had to be an FCM to have TOPS equipment, which allowed brokers to enter an order electronically from anywhere in the world directly to the trading floor instantaneously with their mainframe computers.

A few firms, such as Merrill Lynch, had their own private systems in the 1970s, but TOPS opened the way for more FCMs to participate in getting their orders directly to the floor without the delays involved in having to relay orders. That included introducing brokers when, around 1990, LFG set up a satellite transmission network to allow its IBs, in effect, to become order desks to interface directly into TOPS.

A more recent development to handle orders more efficiently in the open-outcry environment is the CME Universal Broker Station (CUBS), which was first introduced in the CME S&P 500 Index futures pit in April 1997 and has since expanded to other pits. The CUBS unit (actually CUBS2 in 1999) is a laptop computer mounted on a pedestal in the center of a pit. Orders going to TOPS printers, which are now located next to most of the pits in Chicago, New York, and elsewhere, have to be printed out, and an arb clerk outside the pit flashes hand signals to the firm's floor trader in the pit.

A CUBS order goes right to the broker's terminal in the center of the pit; the broker sees your confirmation number when you see it. Aside from the strategic location in the pit, the more important factor is that CUBS is an excellent organizational tool for the floor broker. The terminal gets a live CME quote feed that changes when the CME price boards change and features a fixed horizontal line in the center of the screen. As the buy orders come into the CUBS unit, they show up below the line arranged in order by price. The sell orders come in above the line in order. All market orders come in directly on the horizontal line. A circle on the line contains the quantity factor. If it's green, it's a buy; if it's red, it's a sell.

The CUBS unit's listing of orders in ascending and descending order is the same way a floor broker would normally organize and hold a deck of trading cards, on which physically written buy and sell information has been entered for each order. If a market drops, say, 500 points in half a minute—which can happen a few times a week in the S&P market—the traditional floor broker pulls out his buy deck and physically counts the number of contracts he has to buy until he gets to a price 500 points lower.

Odds are good that by the time he looks up again, a market like this will not have stayed 500 points lower. If it's 600 lower, it's okay to buy the amount he counted. If it's 400 points lower, however, he will be concerned about overfilling and may not fill all orders. In a fast-market condition, a broker is not held liable for not filling an order, but he is held liable for filling a bad order. So if he misfills a quantity, it can't be passed along to a customer. Because a broker only makes $1 to $3 for every contract executed, he is not likely to take on the liability of misfilling an order.

The CUBS unit resolves much of that dilemma. If the market drops 500 points and uncovers buy orders, it will give a green buy signal and a quantity factor of, say, 70 contracts. The broker doesn't even have to look up, but just has to watch his screen to see what the market is doing. If the market ticks to only 450 lower, the quantity factor changes with every tick the market changes, and the broker always knows the exact number of orders to fill. With this technological advance, the CUBS broker can handle perhaps six to eight times more orders than a normal pit broker—and have a lot larger income.

This doesn't guarantee customers will get a fill in a fast-market situation, of course. Once the CUBS order goes from the terminal into the broker's hands, it is competing with every other order in the pit and is subject to the same physical limitations of the broker and the pit as any order is. However, chances for fills are greatly increased when the broker realizes what the numbers in his deck are at any given moment. The only way he makes money is by filling those orders.

Another benefit of CUBS for customers is faster fill reports. One thing that bogs down floor brokers is the endorsement process. Many times, they can fill an order quickly, but they may be so busy they have to put it in their pocket to endorse later so they can keep up with the market. A CUBS fill-reporting unit placed back-to-back with the order-entry unit reduces that problem. After the floor broker has filled an order, a file-reporting clerk in the pit simply presses a button, instantly flipping the order over to the fill-reporting unit with whatever quantity factor and other information is on that order.

Assume the broker fills orders for 70 contracts involving 35 different accounts averaging two contracts each at three different prices to three different houses. All he or the clerk has to do is type in the three different prices and three different houses and press a button. The computer takes care of the distribution function, breaking up the trade according to first-in/first-out exchange regulations. A typical floor broker with five orders at one price isn't likely to look at a time stamp on the order to see when it arrived. With CUBS, if your order is ahead of a 30-lot order and there's a better fill to be had, you are going to get it every time. That is one example of how a computer can level the playing field for individual traders.

Order flow is only one part of making the market more efficient and, therefore, more competitive. As interest in trading increased globally with the addition of the financial futures markets in the 1980s, U.S. exchanges had another concern. They had to find a way to expand the time their markets were open so they could reach into the regular business hours of other time zones around the world, especially the Far East and Europe, if they wanted to attract more business to their exchanges. Just keeping the trading floors open all night was not a cost-effective solution. So in addition to moving orders in and out of the pit, they needed a way to match orders beyond the time constraints of the open-outcry systems. The idea of developing electronic facilities for trading in after-hours (or "overnight," from the U.S. perspective) sessions began to take root.

Electronic trading had been tried by the International Futures Exchange Ltd. in Bermuda (INTEX) in 1984 and the New Zealand Futures Exchange as early as 1985. The CME introduced the Post Market Trading System a month before the stock market crash in 1987, and the CBOT countered later with its own Aurora plan. Those initial electronic startups eventually evolved into Globex at the CME, which was scheduled to start in 1989 but did not make its first trade until 1992, and Project A at the CBOT, which started on a limited basis in 1994 and did not conduct its first overnight session until November 2, 1995.

While the development of Globex and Project A seemed to come rather slowly—and almost reluctantly, from an exchange outsider's perspective—electronic exchanges were popping up internationally, and U.S. equities and options exchanges also were moving rapidly into the electronic era, a potential threat to take

away traders. Beginning in 1995, the growth of the Internet provided another impetus for U.S. futures exchanges to match what
was being accomplished elsewhere with electronic trading.

U.S. futures markets have inched a little closer to true electronic trading as each new stage of Globex and Globex$_2$, Project
A, and ACCESS 2000 at the New York Mercantile Exchange has
unfolded. However, there have been no tales like those at the
MATIF in Paris or in bund trading in Europe. Given the choice
between open-outcry and electronic trading, MATIF traders abandoned the pits virtually overnight and flocked to their computer
screens in 1998. A few months later, the electronic DTB (now
Eurex) in Frankfurt introduced a bund contract and quickly took
the biggest share of the market away from the open-outcry bund
contract traded in London.

MATIF and Eurex were both financially and electronically
oriented from their beginnings, Chicago traders point out, so the
adoption of the electronic format there was not surprising. The
open-outcry method has a much stronger tradition in U.S. futures markets, so the shift to electronic trading has proceeded
cautiously as exchanges protect their members' interests. Even
the technological advances in TOPS and CUBS are designed to
improve and perpetuate the open-outcry trading system.

Yesterday's Young Turks are today's elder statesmen. Today's
challenges for the futures industry continue to have more to do
with innovative processes than innovative products. If open outcry could deliver the best results consistently, there probably
wouldn't be much question that it could go on forever. But the
speed and efficiency of electronic trading make it evident that
the trend in the futures industry is in that direction. How quickly
that move takes place depends primarily on technology.

Just as individual traders face technology glitches, technology has been an obstacle for both futures and equities exchanges,
centering mostly on issues related to too much volume for too
small a pipe. Exchanges maintain some control on volume and
the speed with which they can handle it by regulating the number of terminals they distribute. When more traders and institutions are confident that the exchanges have the capacity to handle
the huge surges in volume that occur occasionally, the transition
to electronic trading will accelerate.

The move of futures exchanges from membership organizations to for-profit corporate structures, begun by the CME in 1999, should facilitate this process by streamlining decision-making and producing changes more quickly in the face of electronic competition.

In a survey conducted by the Futures Industry Association Information Technology Division in early 1999, 33 of the 41 exchanges responding indicated they had an electronic trading system. Half of these have been installed since 1995. The FIA survey showed that a limit order book is the most popular structure. The "book," or database, contains all bids and offers, usually organized by price and time priority on a first-in, first-out basis.

"Some exchanges offer both a limit order and call market structure," the FIA magazine, *Futures Industry*, reported. "Call market is an auction that takes place at a specific time. Liquidity is enhanced because everyone shows up in the same place at the same time. On computerized systems, call markets have a slightly different behavior than typical of an open-outcry market—bids and offers get posted all day and night. At a designated time, the computer reviews the orders, matches them according to a number of well-documented algorithms, and calculates the trade price."

Systems designed prior to 1997 generally require a dedicated terminal provided by the exchange, according to the FIA, but the more recent open-architecture designs allow application program interfaces (APIs) that make it possible for FCMs to access multiple exchanges from one terminal and to add information and analytical programs of their choice.

The whole trading world appears to be in transition, with exchanges and brokerage firms merging, setting up global alliances, trading longer hours, and establishing (or at least discussing) new public, for-profit ownership structures to cope with the potential threat of Electronic Communications Networks (ECNs). The ECNs would like to make online trading the venue of choice for those wanting to bypass traditional brokers and exchanges and have made inroads that have caused existing securities exchanges to expand their trading hours and to make other modifications to compete with the newcomers taking advantage of technology and the Internet.

Instinet, the oldest and largest ECN, and Datek have been matching buy and sell orders for stocks for some time. Other ECNs, such as Island and Global TRADEBOOK and Archipelago, may ultimately do everything a stock exchange does at a fraction of the cost that brokers require. Established exchanges like Nasdaq are looking at new markets, including bonds, and could compete with the CBOT's futures contract. BrokerTec, a consortium of the world's seven largest banks, could produce a market in bonds similar to the interbank market in currencies, with its electronic trading system trading U.S. and European bonds. If these ventures succeed in the securities and financial markets, they not only could provide formidable competition to some areas of futures trading but also could serve as models of technological change that would probably transfer to the futures industry.

The Cantor Exchange was perhaps the first real entity that brought the realization of that possibility to some futures exchanges. With 20,000 screens worldwide, accounting for about half of all the daily business in the cash government securities market, Cantor loomed as a big threat to the CBOT's open-outcry T-bond market, particularly when Cantor received approval in 1998 to trade interest rate and currency futures products. EBS Partnership, an electronic brokerage system for interbank foreign exchange, posed the same kind of threat to the CME's Eurodollar pit with a forward rate agreement product introduced in November 1998.

What might be a threat to one open-outcry exchange looked like an opportunity for another. Cantor's alliance with the Board of Trade of the City of New York opened up the possibility for that exchange to trade financial products, not only establishing a whole new product area for the exchange without requiring pit space but also providing the technology for electronically trading its traditional commodity products, such as coffee, sugar, cocoa, and cotton.

At about the same time these new electronic plans were evolving, however, the Long-Term Capital Management default reminded traders about the importance of counterparty risk, and the creditworthiness of the established exchanges became more attractive to risk-averse traders. In addition, although Cantor had the trading and clearing mechanism, it did not have a distribution network in place with traders and brokers (other than Cantor Fitzgerald) that might be involved in futures trades when it started. Cantor could match the orders electronically, but it still took a phone call for many outside traders to enter an order. Futures exchanges, on the other hand, had access to orders but not the order-matching facilities for most markets.

In spite of the shortfalls some see in today's futures exchanges, it will not be easy for any newcomers to take their place. Any exchange/trading center/ECN has to have (1) products to trade (existing, created, or developed), (2) a pool of participants ready to trade and provide liquidity, (3) an order-handling and matching mechanism that is fair and reliable for all parties (which is where open-outcry exchanges are struggling on heavier volume days), and (4) a clearing function that maintains the integrity of the market. Before you jump into electronic trading elsewhere, you should examine Internet upstarts to see if they have all of those ingredients, especially the fourth one. That's the one distinguishing feature where existing exchanges have a big edge.

eBay and other Internet sites can auction Beanie Babies and just about anything else. The Iowa Electronic Market (**www.biz.uiowa.edu/iem/index.html**) lets you "trade futures" on economic and political events, including elections and Microsoft prices. It is not a regulated "exchange," but it is another example of what is possible electronically. Who's to say a well-capitalized FCM (or consortium) couldn't set up a similar structure to trade futures rather than sitting around waiting for various exchanges going in various directions to decide what they are going to do?

It probably won't be long before someone figures out how to attract traders and trade futures in large volumes consistently and reliably. Whether that happens on the Internet, at an exchange, at an ECN, or at some other new mechanism organized by brokerage firms will likely have a lot to do with the future of today's exchanges and where electronic traders will do their business. Electronic futures trading is the exchanges' game to lose.

Interestingly, both Chicago futures exchanges, once the innovative industry leaders, have reached out to Europe for electronic trading systems to stay in this chase. Below is a guide to what some major futures exchanges are doing with electronic trading.

Even if they are not into electronic trading yet, most exchanges maintain Web sites (see Table 4–1) which are generally among the better sources on the Internet for futures trading information. They usually include typical exchange offerings, such as history, contract specifications, trading statistics, press releases, the chairman's photo and message, and so forth, but they also may include free price quotes and charts, trading tutorials, and other valuable resources. Any electronic trader searching for answers to questions about trading, particularly on specific contracts, should start with an exchange Web site.

CHICAGO MERCANTILE EXCHANGE

The only true electronic futures markets in the United States have been the S&P 500 Index E-mini contract and the more recently added E-mini contracts on the Nasdaq 100 Index and the euro and yen currencies, all traded on the CME's Globex. Other U.S. electronic trading either takes place in after-hours sessions or in side-by-side arrangements where an open-outcry alternative continues to dominate trading activity. Unlike the European experience, the electronic choice in the U.S. has not overwhelmed any open-outcry markets... yet.

When the E-mini S&P was launched on September 9, 1997, the full-sized S&P 500 Index futures contract was valued at $500 times the index, making a total value of about $475,000. At a typical 6 percent or so rate, the minimum initial margin was approaching $30,000 per contract. Even when the contract was split in half to $250 times the index a month or so later, the initial margin of about $15,000 per contract remained a little steep for many traders. Since then, the S&P 500 Index has risen further, taking the value of the futures contract up with it, and the initial margin for the smaller full-size version (symbol SP, $250 times the index) was approaching $25,000 again in mid-1999.

The E-mini S&P (symbol ES) is one-fifth the size of the regular S&P contract. At $50 times the index, the total contract value in mid-1999 was in the $65,000 to $70,000 range, and the initial margin was under $5000 per contract. The average daily range has been around 20 points, or $1000, making it one of the most attractive contracts for a growing number of day traders. It still is not the type of market most should trade with a $5000 beginning account, but it is much more suitable to individual traders who want a stock index component in their portfolio.

The key feature, however, is not the size of the contract but the fact that it is traded electronically on Globex almost 24 hours a day (except from 3:15 p.m. to 3:45 p.m. Chicago time, Monday through Thursday, and 3:15 p.m. Friday until 5:30 p.m. Sunday) and fills are reported within a few seconds. Any E-mini order for 30 contracts or less must be traded on Globex, even during regular trading hours for the S&P 500. During pit trading hours, orders for 31 or more E-mini contracts must be traded via open outcry on an all-or-none basis only.

The other E-mini stock index contract on the Nasdaq 100 Index (symbol NQ), which began trading on June 21, 1999, is also one-fifth the size of the regular contract and parallels the method and hours of trading used for the E-mini S&P. At $20 times the value of the Nasdaq 100 Index, the total contract value was around $45,000 to $50,000 in mid-1999, and the minimum initial margin was about $3500 per contract .

The Nasdaq 100 Index is based on the 100 largest nonfinancial stocks listed on the Nasdaq market, which calculates and disseminates the index under the ticker symbol NDX every 15 seconds during the trading day. With the top 10 stocks in the index leaning to technology and the Internet (Microsoft, Intel, Cisco Systems, MCI Worldcom, Dell Computers, Sun Micro Systems, Amazon.com, Amgen, Level 3 Communications, and Yahoo), the E-mini Nasdaq tends to be more volatile than the S&P 500 and could become a favorite of Internet stock traders as liquidity picks up.

The CME also began electronic trading in its popular Eurodollar contract during regular trading hours on July 6, 1999. Previously, most of the CME's International Monetary Market contracts, including the Eurodollar, were traded in the pits during the day and on Globex overnight. Now, the Eurodollar trades electronically on Globex (symbol GE) side-by-side with open-outcry pit trading (symbol remains ED), giving institutions in Europe the ability to trade real-time without having a floor operation in Chicago.

Eurodollar futures trading on Globex runs from 4:30 p.m. until 4 p.m. the next day Monday through Thursday (Chicago time) and 5:30 p.m. until 4 p.m. Sundays and holidays. The market closes at 4 p.m. on Friday. Regular open-outcry trading hours are 7:20 a.m. until 2 p.m. Daily settlement prices are determined at the end of the open-outcry session, 2 p.m.

Everyone usually refers to the Globex electronic trading system on which all this electronic trading occurs simply as Globex, but it is actually Globex$_2$, developed for the CME by the Paris Stock Exchange (SBF) and its subsidiary, GL Consultants. NSC, the host software, was developed by the SBF, and the servers and clients were developed and integrated with the host by GL, according to the CME's *The Complete Globex$_2$ Handbook*. In addition to the CME, other exchanges using this system include MATIF and the Singapore International Monetary Exchange (SIMEX). The CME has also worked out an alliance with LIFFE.

The open architecture of the system permits APIs with software other than GLWIN, the Globex trading software, the Microsoft Windows NT operating system and Excel spreadsheet program, for example. The GLWIN software provides interfaces to several different exchanges' electronic trading systems and allows traders to customize windows on their screens to their own needs to make them more functional.

The order-matching process is on a first-in, first-out basis, although an allocation algorithm is also used in the Eurodollar futures market.

Traders who want to have the advantage of seeing the "book" can get their own Globex terminal (see Figure 4–1) and can trade on Globex from almost anywhere by becoming an electronic trading holder (ETH). An ETH must have an account with a CME clearing firm, which takes care of administrative functions, credit limits, and other permissioning details. The fees include a $1500 one-time fee, $1000 or so for the dedicated Compaq computer terminal, and a monthly charge of $250, plus clearing fees for each trade. You will also have charges for phone lines, your own information or analytical resources, and the like.

CHICAGO BOARD OF TRADE

The CBOT's alignment with Eurex, approved in mid-1999, could have a significant impact on CBOT electronic trading over the long term. Some industry officials consider the arrangement a positive step because it gives the CBOT access to a proven open-

FIGURE 4–1

Globex Terminal

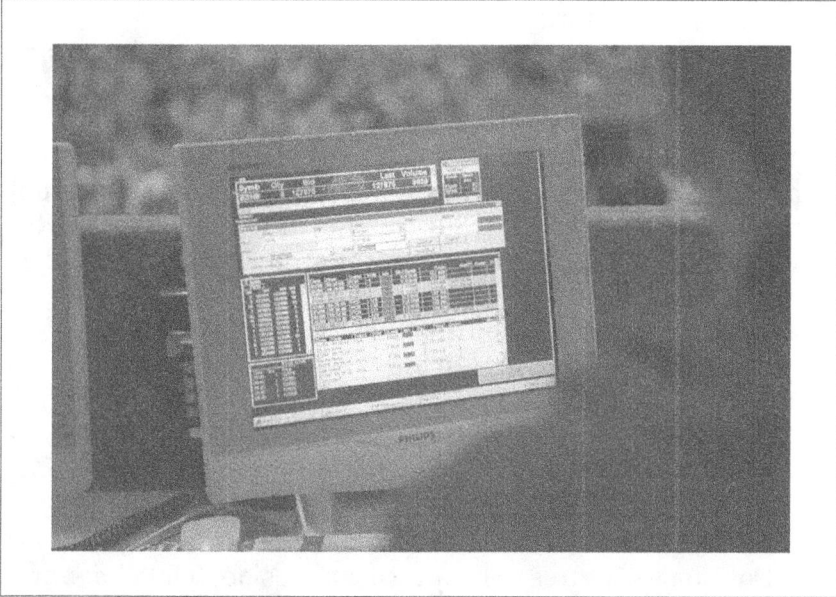

The CME's Globex terminal shows current bid/ask prices and quantities. Windows that log the day's activity feature color-coded orders illustrating their status.

architecture trading platform, so it will not have to update or develop its own. Estimates indicated an extensive upgrade to the CBOT's Project A would cost $47 million, against an estimated $50 million to set up the alliance with Eurex. Considering the Eurex's 5000 terminals in 16 countries, compared with Project A's 700 terminals in four countries, CBOT members, after vacillating over what to do for months, finally decided the link with Eurex looked like the better choice. However, the full implications of the agreement remain to be seen.

Meanwhile, the CBOT continues to use Project A, an electronic order-entry and matching system that allows market participants to trade CBOT financial, agricultural, equity, and electricity futures and options products outside the traditional open-outcry trading hours. Project A has seen some of its busiest periods when market conditions change overnight or over a weekend, such as was the case when weather over the 1999 July 4 holiday weekend caused a surge in Project A trading in corn and other agricultural futures markets.

Expanding the after-hours, overnight trading system to side-by-side trading in T-bonds during regular trading hours has not resulted in much of a shift to the electronic format, however. With strong increases in the number of workstations and participation by firms and locals, electronic trading averaged about a million contracts per month during the first half of 1999, but accounted for only about 5 percent of the total volume at the CBOT. T-bonds represented about two-thirds of the Project A business, with most of that coming during the overnight session.

Project A trading hours (Chicago time) include:

Financial products—day session, 5:30 a.m. until 2 p.m.; afternoon session, 2:15 p.m. until 4 p.m.; overnight session, 6 p.m. until 5 a.m.

Equity products—day session, 5:35 a.m. until 7:50 a.m. for Dow Jones futures only; afternoon session, 3:30 p.m. until 4:30 p.m.; overnight session, 6 p.m. until 5 a.m.

Agricultural products—no day or afternoon sessions; overnight session, 9 p.m. until 4:30 a.m.

Electricity products—day session, 8 a.m. until 2 p.m.; no afternoon or overnight sessions.

Access to Project A is via a Sun workstation provided by the CBOT only to exchange members and member firms exclusively for trading Project A (see Figure 4–2). The Sun terminal is connected to the Project A host (server) via a dedicated line. Dial Access is a service that provides members the ability to access Project A through their personal computer via a private communications network. Rent for the Sun workstation is $300 a month. The network charge is $200 a month in the CBOT building.

In keeping with CBOT policy about not disclosing orders, Project A does not provide traders with a complete "book." Prior to the opening, buy and sell orders are accumulated, using price and the time stamp of the order to arrive at an indicative opening price, which is calculated every 60 seconds. Orders are not

FIGURE 4-2

CBOT Project A Screen

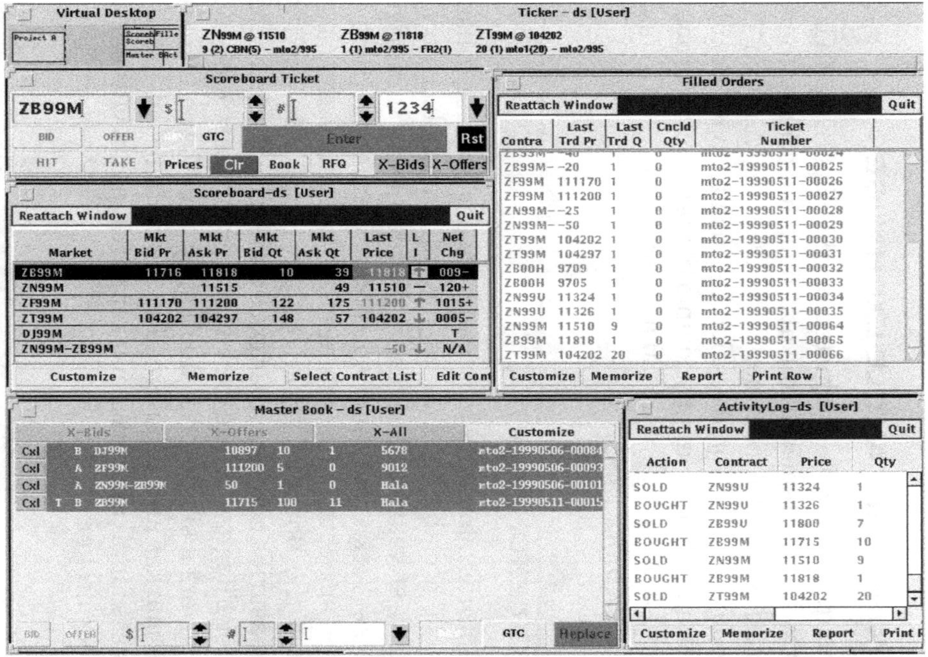

The CBOT's Project A terminal provides a wealth of information, but training is required to understand it all. The Scoreboard window gives bid/ask information, including quantity, and filled orders and activity log windows present a record of what has happened.

matched on a first-in, first-out basis, but an order participation and allocation method rewards size in determining the priority of orders to be filled at a given price. During trading hours, time priority goes to the first order to narrow the bid-ask spread, and order allocation is based on price and quantity in an attempt to simulate what actually happens on the trading floor.

NEW YORK MERCANTILE EXCHANGE

After-hours trading is conducted on the NYMEX ACCESS electronic trading system starting at 4 p.m. and concluding at 8 a.m. the next day (New York time, EST), Monday through Thursday. On Sunday the electronic session begins at 7 p.m. Regular open-outcry trading hours vary by commodity (examples; crude oil, 9:45 a.m. until 3:10 p.m.; gold, 8:20 a.m. until 2:30 p.m.; copper, 8:10 a.m. until 2 p.m.).

CANTOR EXCHANGE

The Cantor Exchange is included here not because it has proven itself to be a viable alternative for individual electronic traders after its first year but because it represents an initiative by the other New York traditional open-outcry exchange that could be emulated elsewhere. It combines the regulatory and clearing expertise of the Board of Trade of the City of New York with the U.S. Treasuries market experience and technological capabilities of Cantor Fitzgerald. The exchange's proprietary electronic platform delivers a single-price auction system to the U.S. Treasury futures market and is designed to promote broad-based and direct access for all approved market participants without the need for a floor broker.

EUREX

Eurex, as mentioned above, is a public company owned equally by Deutsche Börse AG and the Swiss Options and Financial Futures Exchange. In addition to operating the electronic trading platform, Eurex provides an automated and integrated joint clearinghouse for all products and participants, covering the spectrum from trading to final settlement on one electronic trading and clearing platform.

Trading hours (Frankfurt time) for key Eurex contracts include:

Eurobund—8 a.m. until 7 p.m.

The Deutscher Aktienindex (DAX)—futures (euro 25 times the index) and options (euro 5 times the index)—8:25 a.m. until 5 p.m.

Dow Jones STOXX 50 index—(euro 10 times the index)— 10 a.m. until 5 p.m.

Eurex release 3.0, made available to participants in the fall of 1999, added new capabilities in the software architecture with an open interface as well as a modern graphical user interface to more easily inform traders about trade execution and identification.

The VALUES API (Virtual Access Link Using Exchange Services—Application Programming Interface), developed by Eurex in collaboration with Deutsche Börse for the Xetra electronic trading system for the cash market, provides direct, open access to the Eurex network and the Eurex trading system. The programmable interface makes it easier for participants to apply various software options from vendors of their choice as additions or supplements to the standard applications offered by Eurex. Release 4.0, scheduled in 2000, will expand VALUES API to clearing functions.

In addition to financial markets, Eurex is also involved in the German Energy Exchange initiative, a proposal for a new energy exchange set up by Deutsche Börse, Eurex, and NYMEX. Based in Frankfurt, it is to begin electronic trading in 2000.

LONDON INTERNATIONAL FINANCIAL FUTURES AND OPTIONS EXCHANGE (LIFFE)

LIFFE is a prime example of an exchange making the transition from open-outcry to electronic trading. Faced by the prospect of competing against other European exchanges that trade electroni-cally at a time when Europe is moving to one currency, LIFFE put its own electronic trading plan on a faster track and con-verted to screen trading completely on November 29, 1999.

LIFFE CONNECT is LIFFE's electronic trading platform, designed to trade its full range of derivative products. LIFFE committed to the electronic system in June 1998 shortly after the electronic DTB (now Eurex) took the largest share of bund futures trading away from LIFFE's open-outcry floor. The first release of LIFFE CONNECT in November 1998 facilitated the electronic trading of individual equity options. The move to LIFFE CONNECT continued with gilt futures in April 1999, other bond futures in May 1999, short-term interest rates in August 1999, and euro money market contracts in September 1999.

LIFFE CONNECT supports both price/time and pro-rata trade-matching algorithms as well as all LIFFE-recognized strat-egies, including the more complex ones required for short-term interest rates. LIFFE members can access LIFFE CONNECT through one of 16 independent software vendors that have devel-oped front-end packages tailored to suit different trading require-ments. They enable access to LIFFE CONNECT through systems that stand alone or integrate with other front- and back-office systems already in place.

U.S. traders received equal footing with traders elsewhere to access LIFFE CONNECT directly as the result of a no-action letter from the U.S. Commodity Futures Trading Commission (CFTC) in July 1999.

LIFFE CONNECT trading hours (London time) for several key contracts include:

FT-SE 100 Stock Index futures—8:35 a.m. until 6 p.m.

Long gilt futures—8 a.m. until 6 p.m.

Bund futures—7 a.m. until 6 p.m.

Three-month Euribor interest rate futures—regular ses-sion, 7:30 a.m. until 4:10 p.m.; APT session, 4:15 p.m. until 6 p.m.

Three-month sterling interest rate futures—regular ses-sion, 8:05 a.m. until 4:10 p.m.; APT session, 4:15 p.m. until 6 p.m.

SYDNEY FUTURES EXCHANGE

The Sydney Futures Exchange (SFE) is another traditional open-outcry exchange making the transition to an electronic format and may be an example that U.S. floor traders will replicate in the not-too-distant future. The new Windows NT version of SYCOM enables members who have workstations to enter trades directly into the system. An automatic order-entry interface allows members to create their own custom-made routing system that connects directly to the exchange to allow broader access to the market. Clients of a floor member, for example, can access the system from anywhere in the world to become an SFE "local."

TABLE 4—1

Exchange Web Sites

Not every exchange offers electronic trading, but almost all have an Internet site that not only provides information about the exchange and its contracts but also provides useful trading information, links to various resources, and other helpful services for traders. For one of the most complete lists of all exchanges worldwide, check the International Federation of Technical Analysts page at **www.ifta.org/Link-X.htm.**

Country	Exchange	Web Site URL
Argentina	Buenos Aires Futures Exchange	www.matba.com.ar
Australia	Sydney Futures Exchange (SFE)	www.sfe.com.au
Austria	Wiener Börse AG (Vienna)	www.wbag.at
Belgium	Belgian Futures and Options Exchange (BELFOX)	www.belfox.be
Brazil	Bolsa de Mercadorias & Futuros (BM&F) (Sao Paulo)	www.bmf.com.br
Canada	Montreal Exchange	www.me.org
	Toronto Futures Exchange	www.tse.com
	Toronto Stock Exchange	www.tse.com
	Winnipeg Commodity Exchange	www.wce.mb.ca
Chile	Santiago Stock Exchange	www.bolsantiago.cl
Denmark	FUTOP Market-Copenhagen Stock Exchange	www.xcse.dk
Finland	Finnish Options Exchange Ltd. (Helsinki)	www.foex.fi
	Helsinki Securities and Derivatives Exchange (HEX)	www.hex.fi
France	Marche a Terme International de France (MATIF) (Paris)	www.matif.fr
	Marche des Options Negociables de Paris (MONEP)	www.monep.fr

(Continued)

Country	Exchange	Web Site URL
Germany	Eurex Frankfurt	www.eurexchange.com
Greece	Athens Stock Exchange	www.ase.gr
Hong Kong	Hong Kong Futures Exchange	www.hkfe.com
	Stock Exchange of Hong Kong	www.sehk.com.hk
Hungary	Budapest Commodity Exchange	www.bce-bat.com
	Budapest Stock Exchange	www.fornax.hu/fmon
India	National Stock Exchange of India	www.nseindia.com
Israel	Tel Aviv Stock Exchange (TASE)	www.tase.co.il
Italy	Italian Stock Exchange	www.borsaitalia.it
Japan	Kansei Commodities Exchange	//KANEX.OR.JP
	Nagoya Stock Exchange	www.nse.or.jp
	Osaka Mercantile Exchange	www.osamex.com
	Osaka Securities Exchange	www.ose.or.jp
	Tokyo Grain Exchange	www.tge.or.jp
	Tokyo International Financial Futures Exchange (TIFFE)	www.tiffe.or.jp
	Tokyo Commodity Exchange	www.tocom.or.jp
	Tokyo Stock Exchange	www.tse.or.jp
Korea	Korea Stock Exchange (Seoul)	www.kse.or.kr
Malaysia	Commodity and Monetary Exchange of Malaysia (COMMEX Malaysia)	//commex.com.my
	Kuala Lumpur Options & Financial Futures Exchange Bhd	www.kloffe.com.my
Netherlands	Amsterdam Exchanges (AEX)	www.aex.nl
New Zealand	New Zealand Futures & Options Exchange Ltd. (Auckland) (subsidiary of Sydney Futures Exchange)	www.nzfoe.co.nz
Norway	Oslo Stock Exchange	www.ose.no
Peru	Lima Stock Exchange	www.bvl.com.pe
Portugal	Bolsa de Derivados do Porto	www.bdp.pt
	Bolsa de Valores de Lisboa (Lisbon Stock Exchange)	www.bvl.pt
Romania	Bursa Monetar-Financiara si de Marfuri Sibiu	www.bmfms.ro
Russia	The Russian Exchange (Moscow)	www.re.ru
	Inter-Republican Universal Commodity Exchange in Moscow	www.mmb.ru
Singapore	Singapore Commodity Exchange	www.sicom.com.sg
	Singapore International Monetary Exchange Ltd. (SIMEX)	www.simex.com
South Africa	South African Futures Exchange (SAFEX)	www.safex.co.za
	Johannesburg Stock Exchange	www.jse.co.za

Country	Exchange	Web Site URL
Spain	MEFF Renta Fija (Spanish Financial Futures and Options Exchange) (Barcelona)	www.meff.es
	MEFF Renta Variable (Spanish Equity Derivatives Exchange) (Madrid)	www.meffrv.es
	Bolsa de Madrid	www.bolsamadrid.es
Sweden	OM Stockholm AB	www.omgroup.com
	OM Stockholmsbörsen	www.xsse.se
Switzerland	Eurex Zurich AG	www.eurexchange.com
Taiwan	Taiwan Stock Exchange	www.tse.com.tw
Thailand	Stock Exchange of Thailand	www.set.or.th
United Kingdom	International Petroleum Exchange	www.ipe.uk.com
		www.energylive.com
	London International Financia Futures Exchange (LIFFE)	www.liffe.com
	London Metal Exchange (LME)	www.lme.co.uk
	London Stock Exchange	www.stockex.co.uk
United States	American Stock Exchange (AMEX) (New York)	www.amex.com
	Cantor Exchange (New York)	//cx.cantor.com
	Chicago Board Options Exchange (CBOE)	www.cboe.com
	Chicago Board of Trade (CBOT)	www.cbot.com
	Chicago Stock Exchange	www.chicagostockex.com
	Chicago Mercantile Exchange (CME) (includes International Monetary Market, Index and Options Market, and Growth and Emerging Markets divisions, and Globex)	www.cme.com
	Coffee, Sugar & Cocoa Exchange (CSCE) (subsidiary of Board of Trade of the City of New York)	www.csce.com
	Instinet	www.instinet.com
	Kansas City Board of Trade	www.kcbt.com
	MidAmerica Commodity Exchange (MidAm) (affiliate of Chicago Board of Trade)	www.midam.com
	Minneapolis Grain Exchange	www.mge.com
	Nasdaq Stock Market	www.nasdaq.com
	New York Cotton Exchange (NYCE) (subsidiary of Board of Trade of the City of New York; includes FINEX, New York Futures Exchange, Citrus Associates)	www.nyce.com

(Continued)

(Concluded)

Country	Exchange	Web Site URL
	New York Mercantile Exchange (NYMEX) (includes NYMEX and COMEX divisions)	www.nymex.com
	New York Stock Exchange (NYSE)	www.nyse.com
	Pacific Exchange (San Francisco)	www.pacificex.com
	Philadelphia Stock Exchange (PHLX) and Philadelphia Board of Trade	www.phlx.com

CHAPTER 5

Defining Your Style–
Methods for
Electronic Trading

With access to more information, the ability to analyze more data more thoroughly, and the possibility of entering orders faster and more conveniently than ever before, you might assume that everything is now in place for electronic futures traders to start making their fortunes. Only one thing stands in the way: the little matter of actually trading.

Ask anyone who has ever done it and they will tell you that trading futures and options is incredibly difficult to do successfully and consistently. It can be done—it has been done—but to maintain a long-term track record of profits requires a method that works (although it probably requires constant tweaking), the discipline to stick with that method, and a little luck. Even having all those ingredients does not ensure trading success.

Unfortunately, those who are looking to electronic trading as a shortcut to wealth will be disappointed to learn that for the most part, the techniques required to be successful in electronic trading are the same as they are for traditional trading. That is another way of saying that you won't find any more surefire secrets to success by trading electronically than you will by trading the old-fashioned way, according to brokerage firm officials who have observed thousands of customers trading both online and via phone. "If there were one short-term approach that always worked, there wouldn't be any bus drivers," one quipped.

One point that deserves emphasis again about electronic futures trading is that traders may be expecting too much too soon. As you have already read, futures trading has been enhanced by technological advances in many areas, but except for a few markets, it is still essentially an open-outcry marketplace in the United States. Whatever methods or ideas that have been applied to trading in the past still apply today.

As the number of markets traded electronically increases, traders will be able to get into and out of positions quickly and can apply their analytical techniques on a short-term basis. In markets such as the E-mini stock indexes, a one-minute bar chart looks about the same as a daily chart in other markets. However, as a reflection of swings in the psychology of the marketplace, the familiar chart patterns and indicators develop much more quickly on the short-term charts and require quick thinking and quick trading.

If you want to trade a couple of times a week, the only part of electronic trading that may interest you is the information you can access online, described in the pretrade analysis chapter. If you want to take advantage of online trading to be a more active trader, however, you need a thorough understanding of how to place orders first. Then you can consider methods you can use to trade in an electronic environment.

STOPS AND OTHER ORDERS

Logic suggests that one area where the self-directed online trader should excel is in understanding and placing orders. However, brokerage firm officials report that one of the big problems for many newcomers to online trading is that they enter orders incorrectly. They may be able to express to a broker what they want to do, but to put their wishes into a couple of fields on an online order form may not be so easy or may be complicated by the fact that they simply do not know the format for the price in which their market is quoted. What a customer wants to accomplish might be done with a limit order, but he may not be sure of the procedure or the price format. So instead of the limit order he actually wants, he just puts in a market order and takes what he gets.

Even though all online brokers claim that their system is "simple" and "easy" to use, order entry is not always so easy and intuitive until you get enough experience to become comfortable with the way your broker wants an order presented. The process is complicated by the fact that data services, brokerage firms, and exchanges do not always use the same symbol for a contract or the same way to state price quotes. In fact, one of the challenges facing the futures industry in general is that there does not seem to be a standardized way to do anything. If you plan to enter orders online yourself without a broker to guide you, you should become proficient in order terminology and familiar with every nuance of an order and what happens to it when it hits the marketplace, whether that's on the trading floor or on a terminal.

Several brokerage firm officials report another order-entry problem that you would not expect from electronic traders, who may analyze their trades carefully: Too many traders just walk away from their terminal after hitting "submit," assuming everything will happen automatically now that they are entering orders online. Brokers advise traders to always check their screen after an order has been submitted. The order can be rejected for any number of reasons—bad price, wrong order type, not enough margin to cover that extra 0 that slipped into the quantity of contracts in the order, you name it. The trader, however, thinks he has a position because he didn't bother to check his fills or working orders. Then he places a stop based on that order, and the market hits his stop. Now, he has a position in the direction he did not want and no position in the direction he did want.

With the current technology in futures trading, brokers advise that you never assume anything when it comes to order entry. Watch for confirmations and fills so you know your status.

You can find the following information on the Internet sites of many of the brokers listed in the chapter on brokerage firms, but here is a brief overview of what the electronic trader should know about the orders used most often.

Market Order

A market order is the most frequently used order. It does not specify a price and is executed at the best possible price available at the time it hits the floor. In a liquid market, this gets you in or out of a position without having to chase the market, but in a thin market, it leaves you vulnerable to being filled far from the current price. Some traders say they never use market orders; some use them all the time.

For today's electronic trader, who often must move quickly, using a market order depends on the market, the current situation, and your desire to have a position. If you really want to be in or, more important, out of a market, use market orders and don't try to be too cute (assuming you are trading liquid markets). Once a market order is in the system, it cannot be cancelled.

Limit Order

A limit order is an order to buy or sell at a designated price. A limit order to buy is placed below the current price. A limit order to sell is placed above the current price. The limit order tells the floor broker you want action at a specified price, but it does not guarantee that your order will be executed, even if your data service shows the market traded at your price. The floor trader may not have been able to fill the order at the price you designated.

Or Better

Or better is like a market order with a limit. The floor trader is obligated to get the best possible price for the customer. That may turn out to be better than the limit order price requested.

Market If Touched (MIT) Order

An MIT order is similar to a limit order in several respects. A buy MIT is placed below the current price, a sell MIT is placed above the current price, and the order includes a specific price. However, once that specified price is touched or passed through, an MIT order becomes a market order, meaning the execution may be at, above, or below the price you designated. An MIT order is usually used to enter the market or initiate a trade.

Stop Order

One of the first rules newcomers to futures trading hear is to use stops. The stop order isn't foolproof, but its most familiar use is to get you out of a losing position when a specified price is hit. In addition to minimizing a loss, a stop order can also be used to take a profit or as a way to initiate a new position.

A buy stop is placed above the current price. A sell stop is placed below the current price. Once the stop price is touched, the order is treated like a market order and will be filled at the best possible price. As with a market order, that price can be far from the stop price you designated. If you entered a sell stop just below the previous close and the market opens limit down, you could be filled at limit down—or maybe even several limit downs if no buyer steps up to take your order. Stops can be tricky, but most traders cannot afford to trade without them.

Spread Order

Basic spread orders can be between different contract months of the same market, between two related markets, or between related markets traded on different exchanges. The goal is to capitalize on changes in the price differential or spread between the two contracts by buying one and selling the other. Typically, worthwhile changes in price relationships take time to develop, so spreads may not be attractive to the short-term electronic trader. However, there may be circumstances when temporary price distortions provide spreading opportunities with reduced risk.

Most firms have special areas on their order-entry screens where you can enter spread orders at the market or can designate that you wish to be filled when the price difference between the markets reaches a certain point (or premium). As with limit orders, seeing the price differential you specified on your quote screen does not mean the floor broker was able to fill your spread order at the designated price. Physical factors, such as the location of the two pits, or a limited number of contracts traded at a price may get you an "unable" report, even when it appears your spread could have been filled.

Although spreads usually involve a buy and a sell situation, today's more sophisticated strategies using options may involve two buys or two sells or various other arrangements in "strangles," "butterflies," or other positions with the potential to become very complex and confusing very quickly. For this reason, some firms restrict their customers' ability to enter options spreads online. These orders are not for the inexperienced trader, online or otherwise.

Other Orders

A number of other specialized order possibilities are available, but they may be of limited usefulness to most online traders, particularly without a broker's assistance.

Stop Limit Order

The first part of a stop limit order is like the stop order described above, but it includes a second price that specifies the limit at which you want your stop filled. Your sell stop order may indicate a 510 stop, limit 505. If the market trades at 504, the order will not be filled and you still have your long position. It is usually not a good idea to use a stop limit order when you are trying to exit a position.

Stop Close Only Order

This stop will be triggered only if the market touches the specified price during the close of trading. In a fast-market situation and a hectic close, that may not be a favorable price, but this type of order does keep you from getting filled at the price if the market fluctuates wildly and spikes up or down during the trading session.

Market on Opening (MOO)

This order is executed during the opening range of trading at the best possible price within the opening range. The Chicago Board of Trade is one exchange that does not recognize this order.

Market on Close (MOC)

Also known as "murder on close," this order will be filled during the final minutes of trading at whatever price is available. Its nickname describes its impact at times.

Fill or Kill (FOK)

This order tells the floor broker to buy or sell at a specific price and if that is not possible, to cancel the order. A broker may make, say, three attempts, and if no one bites, the order is killed.

One Cancels the Other (OCO)

This order combines two orders on one ticket, telling the floor broker that once one side of the order is filled, the other side of the order should be cancelled. Putting the two orders together eliminates the possibility of a double fill. This type of order is not accepted on all exchanges.

Day Orders

These orders are active from the time they enter the trading pits until the close of that day only. Order prices are usually fairly close to the current price.

Good 'Til Cancelled (GTC), or Open Orders

Open orders are active from the time they enter the pits until you cancel them, they are filled or the contract expires. Order prices are normally a little distant from current prices. A trader needs to be cautious about placing resting open orders that just sit there for a long time. It is easy to forget about them and then be surprised when they are filled later.

Fast Market

This is not an order but a market condition that means orders are "not held." In other words, in chaotic conditions when the market is moving rapidly, orders might not be filled or might be filled long after the price desired was triggered.

ELECTRONIC TRADING APPROACHES

We have already stressed that many different approaches can be used to trade futures successfully in any time frame and that the methods aren't that much different in an electronic setting. One of the attractions of short-term trading is that you can take advantage of technology and electronic order-matching facilities to apply your techniques and capture significant profits with potentially less risk in a shorter amount of time.

We are not advocating day trading specifically, particularly the scalping techniques to pick up a tick or two that have been widely publicized—and criticized—in the stock market. In the past, day trading futures from off the trading floor was virtually impossible, and certainly not recommended, because of the time lags in getting price information and in getting fill reports on your orders. Today, however, real-time price data is readily available, and your orders can be entered and executed almost instantaneously in markets where electronic order-matching is available. Online trading is not the same thing as day trading, but for many day trading has become an attractive alternative to holding positions overnight.

Figure 5–1 illustrates one of the risks in traditional position futures trading. After an extended downtrend, the November 1998 soybean contract rallied in early October. When prices closed above the previous high, that would have been enough to produce a buy signal on many systems, whether that was the result of simple technical analysis, a moving average, or some other criteria. If you bought immediately on the breakout to a new high during the day, you were well-positioned for what was to come. However, many systems would not have generated a buy signal until the closing price was known. By then, of course, it was too late to buy in the regular trading session.

When the U.S. Department of Agriculture released a surprising crop report figure the morning after the signal, the market opened limit up—30 cents higher, or $1500 per contract. If you had placed a market order to buy on the open based on your system's signal, you were filled 30 cents higher than you expected and the market went down from there. If you had decided to hold off your buy order until after you saw the crop report, you were spared. But whether you got in or not, your trading system software may say you were long at the point of the signal, and the system's performance report shows you made a big profit on the crop report surprise.

A locked limit up or limit down open has always been one of the risks of futures trading. Whenever a market is closed, buying or selling pressure can build up if a new development warrants a change in market attitude. When you combine a closed market and a surprise event, the price response when the market does open can be quite spectacular and beyond your control. In some markets, it seems like most of the price change occurs overnight in circumstances like this, which are difficult to trade. Whether

FIGURE 5–1

A Risk of Traditional Position Futures Trading

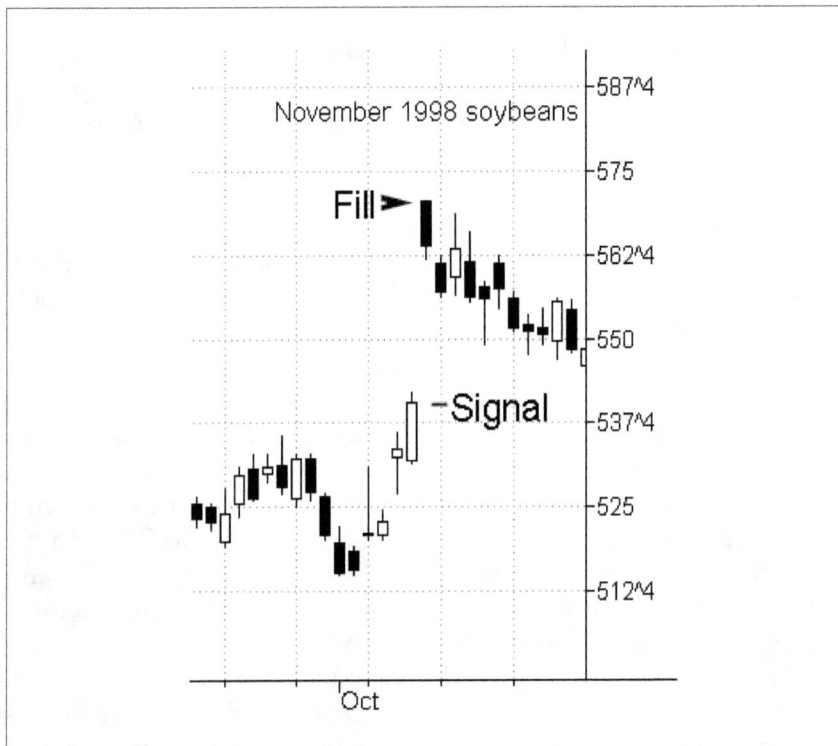

November 1998 soybeans

Fill

−Signal

587^4
575
562^4
550
537^4
525
512^4

Oct

Source: Omega Research's SuperCharts using Commodity Systems Inc. data.

it is a weather market in grains or a bank announcement in Europe affecting financial markets, holding positions overnight or over a weekend can involve a great deal of risk. Of course, if you guess right and have the right position, the rewards can also be huge.

Globex, Project A, ACCESS, and other electronic systems now make it possible to take positions when the trading floors are closed, but trading remains comparatively thin in sessions outside regular trading hours. Rather than take on that risk in uncertain situations, some traders have decided that it is safer to trade only within the regular trading session and not to maintain positions overnight.

This day trading approach certainly doesn't eliminate risk. Ask anyone who had a short stock index position around 2:30 p.m. (CST) on another afternoon in October 1998 when Federal Reserve Chairman Alan Greenspan announced a surprising interest rate cut, or look at the charts when employment numbers or some other economic data are released early in the trading day. These instances show that prices can also change dramatically during a regular trading session. That means risk, but it also means opportunity for a nimble trader in a liquid market.

With electronic trading, the day trading strategies that once were limited only to floor traders have now become available to a much wider audience trading in front of computer screens in their homes or offices. Day trading is now worth a look for anyone wanting to be an active futures trader.

So how can day traders look at the market? The following methods might be useful to an electronic trader, if (1) the market is liquid, (2) your orders can be filled promptly at or very close to the price you determine, and (3) you have the ability to make quick decisions. These examples are based on the S&P 500 Index E-mini contract, which started trading in September 1997 and has become one of the most active contracts at the Chicago Mercantile Exchange. Almost any day could have been selected for illustrative purposes because the contract features a wide enough average daily trading range to produce viable returns within the day and often has several tradable trends during a trading session.

Trade Within a Trending Channel

Trade with the trend is such an ingrained rule in trading that you would think there is no other alternative if you want to be successful. There are other approaches, but following the trend is clearly the method of choice for most traders. For electronic traders, that usually means short-term trends that may or may not be in line with the overall longer-term market trend.

Charts provide a picture of market psychology, and trendlines and channels reveal the intensity of the crowd's mood. The degree of bullishness or bearishness is reflected by how far and how fast the crowd takes prices higher or lower. When a move gets under way, it tends to persist at the same rate of momentum until the buying demand or the selling pressure diminishes or dries up. That is particularly true in intraday trading, when traders get caught up in the action of the marketplace and try to stay in tune with the crowd.

In a rising market, experienced traders advise going with the flow, and buying strength is a better strategy than trying to buy a dip or trying to pick a top to sell short. Putting a buy order below the market is more of a prayer than it is a strategy, asserts one trader. Some traders have criteria for what constitutes a rising or declining channel based on a percentage of the previous day's true range. The important factor in this approach is to find the trend channel and stay with it until it isn't the trend.

Figure 5–2 is a one-minute bar chart of the S&P 500 Index futures contract in the first hour of trading one mid-summer 1999

FIGURE 5–2

A Trending Channel

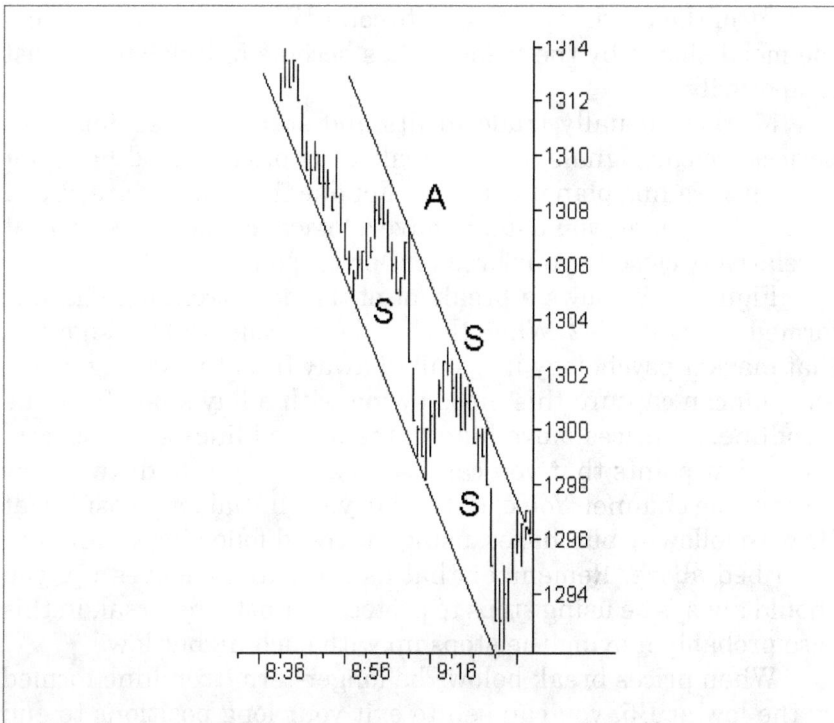

Source: Omega Research's SuperCharts using BMI data.

day. For those inclined to trade with the trend, especially if the longer-term trend is in the same direction, this downtrending channel offered several points to sell (S) once the trendline (A) and channel were established. An electronic trader assuming the downward action would continue and in a position to get out quickly if it didn't could have sold whenever the market broke below previous lows or could have sold the test of the trendline at 1300 when it appeared the trendline would hold. It looks pretty easy in hindsight, naturally, but spotting channels in time to trade the stair-step price action is usually not so simple in the heat of trading.

Trade a Channel Breakout

Trading within a channel can be tricky because you can assume a trend will continue, but you can't read the market's willingness to extend the trend at its current pace. What is more noticeable is when prices break out of a channel, indicating that the psychology of the market participants collectively has changed from the mood shown by the trend or has become indecisive, at least temporarily.

Markets usually trade in fits and starts and seldom give perfectly clear signals, but a breakout is often a good basis for putting a trading plan into action. For one thing, if you are wrong in your judgment, you usually have a logical place for a stop that is relatively close to your breakout entry point.

Figure 5–3 shows a breakout of the downtrending channel formed in Figure 5–2. When the breakout occurs (B1), it signifies that market psychology has shifted away from the selling mode, and you can capture this mood swing with a buy stop above the trendline. As prices move higher, the dashed lines show several higher low points that you can use in an attempt to draw a new uptrending channel. You could add to your initial long position at B1 with followup purchases, using the trend-following techniques described above. Remember that as the market moves up, you should always be using stops to protect against a reversal, in this case probably moving the stops up with each higher low.

When prices break below the longer-term trendline formed by the low at B5, you can sell to exit your long positions to end

FIGURE 5–3

A Channel Breakout

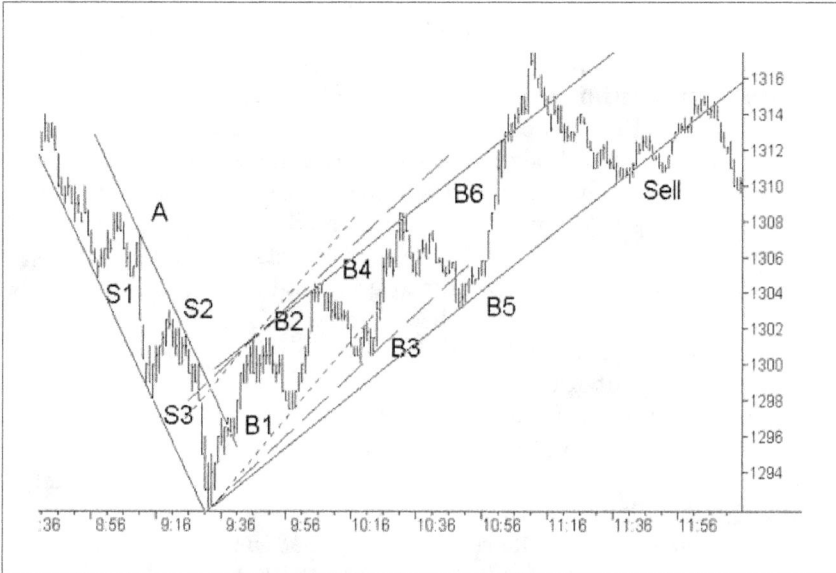

Source: Omega Research's SuperCharts using BMI data.

this "campaign" and either quit for the day or look for a new channel to form to reflect the next stage of market psychology.

Trade an Opening Range Breakout

When the regular trading session opens and traders have more orders to sift through, prices may move up or down erratically as the orders are filled. Eventually—maybe 10 minutes or maybe 30 minutes, depending on the day—the market tends to settle down and begins to move in one direction or the other. If you place a buy stop above the opening range high and a sell stop below the opening range low, you can get onboard a trend as it begins and have your stop in place at the most logical point. If prices stay within the opening range and the market drifts sideways, you may not want to have a position anyway.

Markets have a way of not always making it work that smoothly, however. Price spikes up or down may stop you into or

PAINFUL "PRACTICE"

I know from personal experience that the market can make some unusual errors. Normally, the S&P 500 E-mini tracks the full-size S&P futures contract very closely. On one occasion, I had a short position in the E-mini contract at 1309 and placed a protective buy stop at 1316, well above the market's trading range. Watching price action in the full-size S&P, the market never got above 1312. However, somebody at a brokerage firm, thinking he was placing practice trades in a simulated trading mode, entered several orders to buy a large number of E-mini contracts. As the buy orders came in, they caused the E-mini to spike up to 1316, stopping me out. When the brokerage firm discovered its mistake, it sold the E-mini contracts quickly, contributing to a plunge that took the market down to about 1300.

The aberration caused by the brokerage firm error not only gave me an actual $350 loss per contract but also wiped out my chance for a $450 profit after I had positioned myself correctly for just such a move. The brokerage firm also paid dearly for its mistake.

For those who had sell orders resting at 1315 or 1316 but didn't expect them to be filled with the S&P at 1312, it was a bonanza.

The lesson learned is that ES is not SP, that is, the E-mini S&P is not the S&P 500 Index contract. It is an independent and separate contract. The two usually do track each closely, but strange things can and do happen in the markets occasionally. And, of course, in the end there is another trading axiom that applies: *The market is always right*—even when it does some weird things.

out of positions as the market tests the limits of the range, or the market may "make a mistake." Larry Williams, one of the best-known futures traders and author of numerous books on trading, even made famous a little trading strategy based on a market mistake. He called it "Oops," for good reason, because the market, after starting in one direction, appears to recognize it has made a mistake and goes back the other way. In the Oops tactic, if the market opens below the previous day's low and then rallies, buy at the previous day's low if the price rallies back to that point. If the market opens above the previous day's high and then slips, sell at the previous day's high if the price declines to that point.

Trade Support/Resistance

The setup for this approach is similar to the opening range breakout above. However, instead of buying the breakout above a sideways range, you sell when prices approach resistance at the top of the trading range. Instead of selling the breakout below a sideways range, you buy when prices approach support at the bottom of the trading range.

Depending on prior market action and your judgment about the market's next move, you might conclude that prices are not likely to move above or below a certain level. On Figure 5–4, for example, your analysis might lead you to believe that the market will not get above resistance at 1312. As prices test that level and back off several times, you might regard that as evidence your opinion is correct and sell as prices reach resistance again.

You could come to a similar conclusion to buy, using support at the bottom of the range as your launching point for a long position. You might not be correct, of course, but the advantage of electronic trading is that you can get out of a position quickly

FIGURE 5–4

Trading Support and Resistance

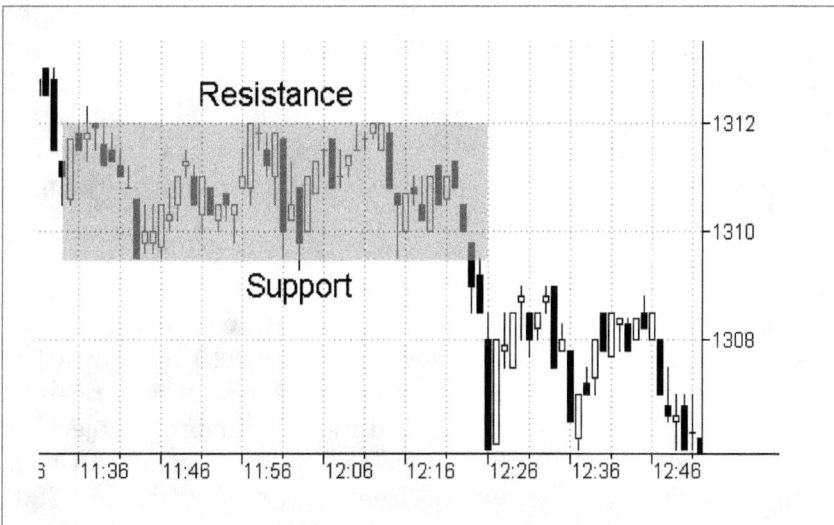

Source: Omega Research's SuperCharts using BMI data.

with a small loss if the market breaks out above the range if you are short or below the range if you are long. As long as you have the flexibility to reverse your thinking and keep your losses at a minimum, you have the opportunity to catch the real move when it does occur.

Trade Reactions to Events or Reports

Don't try to anticipate events or reports, but use overreactions to them to establish a short-term position. When you *know* what a report will say, it's likely that everyone else will know, too, if it's that obvious. The market thrives on surprises, when an actual number is beyond the range of what most traders expected or when the actual number fails to live up to trade expectations.

Figure 5–5 illustrates this type of situation. After trading in the overnight session around 1326 (box A), the S&P 500 Index plunges from that level shortly after 7:30 a.m. when a U.S. government report is released. It may have been retail sales or employment numbers or some other economic report, but traders clearly interpreted it as bearish for the stock market.

After waffling around on Globex in preopening trade, S&P 500 Index futures start the regular trading session about 15 points lower than the previous day's regular session close. The decline may very well turn out to be justified in the long run, but in the immediate aftermath of a report, the market often tends to overdo its reaction. Like a rubber band that has been stretched too far, the market is likely to snap back to a more normal situation before it decides what it will do next. An opportunistic trader who can move very quickly may be able to capitalize on this temporary situation.

Placing a buy stop above the opening range (box B), you would have gotten long about 1314, putting a sell stop below the opening range at about 1310 or so to protect you in case the market did decide to continue going down (a $200 risk). Within a few minutes after buying at 1314, your return could have been as much as $800 per contract, depending on your profit objective. Assuming you waited and sold at S when the market fell back from its corrective rally, you still would have realized about $200 per contract.

FIGURE 5–5

Trading Market Reactions to News

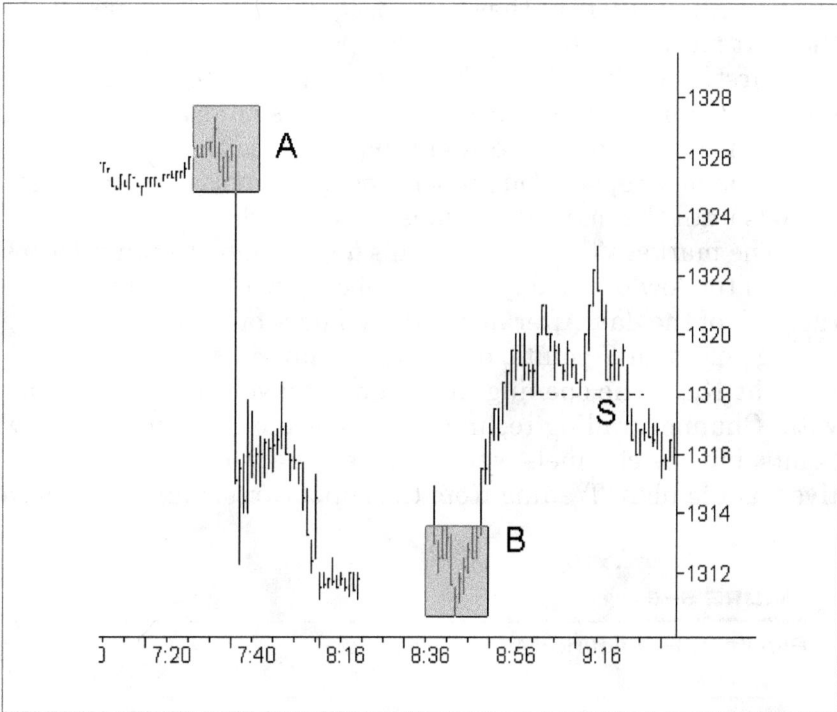

Source: Omega Research's SuperCharts using BMI data.

This can be a tough trade to make, psychologically, because the news that has just come out and the traders' initial reaction are both so bearish and you are going in the opposite direction. What if the world is right and you are wrong? It can be very risky to go against the prevailing mood. For some traders, this may be a "plunge" and a time to panic and unload long positions. For others, this situation may be a "dip" and a buying opportunity to accumulate more positions.

The Flexible Electronic Approach

Electronic trading won't make you a smarter trader, whatever method you use. It just gives you a chance to act quickly and, more important, to react more quickly to reduce your losses in case you are wrong.

Figure 5–6 provides an example of the dilemma that frequently faces traders as they try to decipher charts for clues about the next market direction.

First, note the price spike (A) that occurs about an hour before the regular trading session opens. It is an example of what can happen in thinner overnight market conditions in response to an economic report. You probably should avoid trading in these periods until the market becomes more liquid.

The market's first move on this day is higher; then it comes back to the low of the day. Next, it moves back up to just above the high of the day. After about three hours of trading, you have a range of about 7 points, defined by support at 1306 and resistance at 1313. The opening range did not give you much to work with. Channel trading techniques might have gotten you a few points, but the channels were too steep and volatile for an effective trading plan. Trading from the support/resistance approach

FIGURE 5–6

Pitfalls of Predicting Market Direction

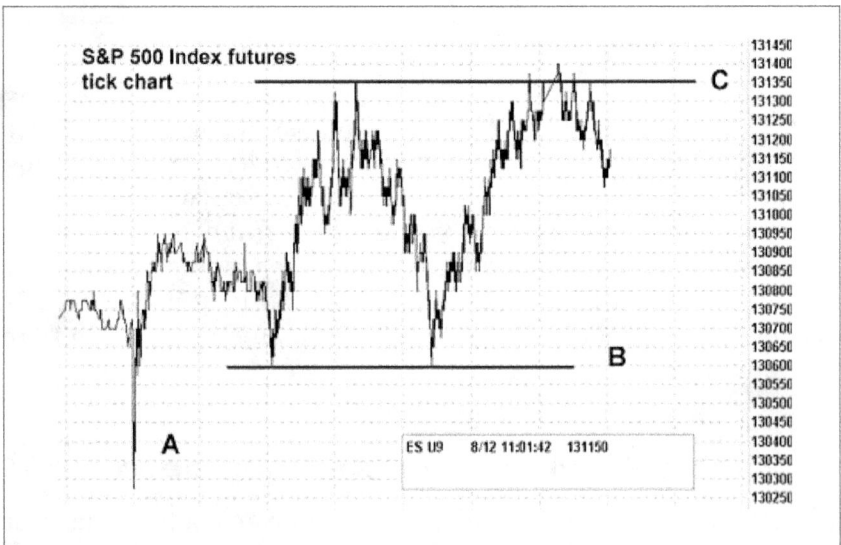

Source: eSignal, Data Broadcasting Corp.

FIGURE 5–7

The Magic of Hindsight

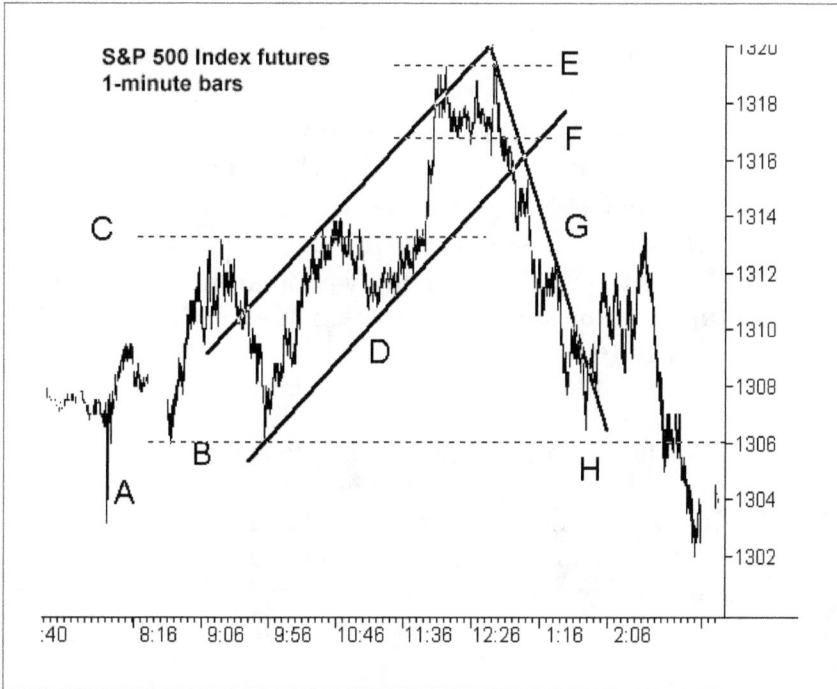

S&P 500 Index futures
1-minute bars

Source: eSignal, Data Broadcasting Corp.

would have been pretty much a guess unless prior market action showed those areas to be significant.

It's halfway through the trading day, and you haven't reached your $500 a day trading goal. Do you pack it up and come back another day? Or do you keep trying to solve this day's trading mystery?

Through the magic of hindsight, Figure 5–7 shows there was plenty of profit potential that day, depending on how you traded it.

1. You might have concluded that B was indeed a good support area and bought around 1306.

2. You might have bought the breakout above resistance at C in the 1313.50 area.

3. You might have exited the long positions on the break below the E–F trading range around 1317.

4. You might have exited the long positions or gone short for a new position on the break below the trendline formed by the lows at B and D in the 1315 vicinity.

5. You might have ridden the new trendline (G) down with the short position until it approached the support line (B) and hit the low (H) just above 1306.

6. You might have exited the short position when the trendline (G) was broken around 1309.

7. Using the market's money, you might have been more inclined to ride out the correction after the low at H and gotten out of the short position on the close at around 1303.

That is a lot of "might haves" to go along with the "couldas" and "shouldas" and "if onlies" that traders often use to describe their trading experiences after the fact. We are not trying to defend or recommend any trading method over another; we are simply trying to point out that the electronic trader has a number of different ways to view and adapt to market conditions every day.

Will They Last?

In the excitement about electronic trading, the E-mini stock index contracts have become quite popular and are sometimes considered to be the prototype for the future of electronic futures trading. But that could change in a different stock market environment, and electronic traders may want to think more broadly than just that one area.

"Keep in mind that the E-mini contracts happen to be the markets that the retail client is trading right now," notes Tom Zabroske, president of DH Financial in Chicago. "Every market has a life span relative to the demand from the retail market to trade it. We have seen this in the past when such markets as the T-bill, silver, gold, etc., had their heyday.

"However, given the extreme margins for the E-mini contracts, retail clients can achieve the same opportunities in other markets and give themselves the ability to trade multiple contracts," Zabroske points out. "As it stands right now, most E-mini traders trade a one- or two-lot—that is, they only have one or two bullets to shoot, and once shot, they are out of ammo. For the same amount of margin money as an E-mini, a client can trade 10 contracts of corn and have a lot more shots/bullets with which to trade.

"The opportunity and/or volatility of the smaller markets do not match the S&P on a one-to-one ratio," he continues, "but once the trader has 10 contracts of a lower-margined contract, the opportunity and volatility are as great, if not greater. There are many markets that can provide the client the opportunity to avoid bringing a knife to a gunfight."

CHAPTER 6

Trading Rules for Electronic Traders

Traders love trading rules, those catchy little sayings that pack both wit and wisdom. They don't always remember the rules when they get caught up in the emotion of trading, but the axioms and clichés they remember the best are those that have been repeated thousands of times and apply today as much as they did to traders years ago.

Because electronic trading still means open-outcry trading for most U.S. markets, the trading rules for electronic trading are the same rules that have always applied to futures trading—with a twist or two to cover the short-term duration of most electronic trades. The overriding concerns will continue to revolve around key words like control, planning, discipline, risk management... That hasn't changed just because traders now have access to more information on the Internet and can transmit their orders electronically.

The traders who have the best odds of succeeding are the ones who understand how the markets work and how the pits operate. Candidates for failure are those who are undercapitalized, do not comprehend the power of leverage, and do not realize how different stocks are from futures in such basic details as how margins are calculated and collected.

Although changes in processing information and orders will undoubtedly require some adjustments, futures trading will remain primarily a psychological game, whether traders are standing on a trading floor or sitting in front of a computer screen. The way they implement their tactics may change a little, but the personal traits and principles that made a trader successful yesterday will continue to be the same tomorrow. Electronic trading is just a delivery mechanism to help market participants accomplish the goal of making money or hedging risk or being right or whatever other trading goals they may have.

Some of the following rules apply specifically to markets where true end-to-end electronic trading is taking place. Others reiterate traditional trading rules with an electronic perspective.

Control your trading situation.

This rule involves all facets of trading, but for the electronic trader, it carries a special emphasis to control technology or the communication link to the trading world. Until technology becomes totally reliable, this may be one of the biggest challenges for an electronic trader. Brokerage firms and exchanges have made it very clear that traders are responsible for their own trading accounts, even if it is the exchange or broker computer systems that fail.

Therefore, you need to control everything over which you can have control to have all your connections in place—the phone lines or satellite system, the data service, the Internet service provider, etc.—so you can trade confidently. Clarify with your brokerage firms what the policies are for errors and mistakes when communication is disrupted for any reason. Get the firm's emergency 800 backup number so you can verify orders if the need arises.

Many things can and do happen to the thread that ties an electronic trader to the marketplace. These are risks that traders are not likely to experience using only the phone. Keep as many of them under your control as you can if you expect to have open positions.

Control your trading.

If you are trading serious money, trade it seriously. One of the dangers of electronic trading is that it can become addictive because of its instantaneous results; press a button and watch the market spin, just like watching a slot machine at a casino. Such impulsive behavior can be the biggest threat to electronic trading accounts for traders who are not prepared to keep this urge under control. Don't overtrade your capital or your trading skills. The electronic trader who thinks technology is the solution to figuring out every trade will probably need to have more discipline than the traditional trader to stay within her or his limits.

One of the biggest concerns brokerage firms have today is the turnover rate in customers. At one firm, an official says the trading life of a full-service account is about a year, a discount account about six months, and an electronic account only three to three and a half months. The electronic account trades about two to two and a half times as much as the average account.

Electronic trading may be easy and exciting, but it can have a costly side to it.

Control your trading II.

This is probably more of a byproduct of a weakness in technology than it is a weakness in trading. As a computer user, you probably have experienced a time when you sent a document to the printer and nothing seemed to happen. You hit print again and still nothing. Then you may try changing your settings or making some other adjustment before hitting print again. You want one printout, but before you know it, you have the same file lined up five times in your printer queue.

The same type of thing sometimes happens with new electronic traders. They punch in an order and hit "submit." If they see the order sitting there, they may have forgotten they sent it and hit "submit" again. Or they may not spot it immediately on the working orders page and think, "Hmm, the system must have been down. I'll send it again." As long as there is enough margin money and the orders are within acceptable parameters, they may pile up in the system until the trader suddenly has a position way beyond his control. That can also happen with stops, where you intend to get out of one position but wind up with an unwanted position in the opposite direction because you placed the stop several times to be sure you would get out.

Punching buttons on a computer is always tricky, especially when you don't know the consequences of a given action, and in electronic trading it can be expensive.

Plan your trade and trade your plan.

This cliché may seem difficult to implement in an electronic setting, in which markets often move so fast that you don't have a lot of time to lay out an elaborate plan. However, you should have a basic trading plan and apply it to trading situations as they develop. Banks require a business plan for you to use their money;

you should be as diligent when it comes to using your own money. After all, trading—online or otherwise—is a business, and it takes time to develop the skills to be successful at it. You have to build a foundation for your trading and then, hopefully, become consistent enough soon enough so you don't become a burnout victim. That can happen to any prospective trader who does not educate herself and does not develop a trading plan, but an electronic environment just makes it happen faster.

On the other hand, faced with the need to plan versus the desire to trade, you may come up with a great plan but too late for the market. "A plan without action is a dream," one industry leader has pointed out, so you need to have a basic plan in place that is both simple and effective and can be tailored to fit the current situation. You don't want to be caught dreaming when your type of market conditions arrive.

Discipline, discipline, discipline.

Everyone acknowledges discipline is most important, but achieving it requires, well, discipline. Just how to get it is another one of those perplexing heredity/environment questions. Are you born with discipline as an innate characteristic, or can you develop discipline through training or personal will power? Playing a musical instrument or a sport or being involved in some other activity in your daily life may help you improve your discipline, but this is an ongoing debate we will leave for the psychologists.

We will just go on record by saying that bad habits tend to lead to bad trading. If you are a procrastinator who waits for something to happen, chances are that trait will be magnified in your trading habits. You may hold on to losers waiting for them to turn profitable, for example.

To be successful, online traders often must think and act quickly without stopping to worry about their discipline. As a trader, you must have confidence in yourself, your data, your analysis, your electronic connections, and your trading method and system. You need the will to stick with your method and, more important, the ability to take the loss when it is wrong. With a number of short-term positions and rapid price fluctuations, electronic traders particularly have to have discipline to survive. "When I lose money, it is always because I fudged on discipline," one electronic trader told us.

Know your market.

If you do your own research and enter your orders online, you do not have a broker backing you up to catch your mistakes (unless they are so bad that the system rejects your orders). The biggest problem brokers say they have with traders is inexperience and lack of preparation. Customers get into a market they do not understand; they may not know how prices for their market are quoted; they may not understand the different types of orders, etc. Even many who have invested in stocks for years and know all about "trading" do not understand futures. Futures are not stocks, and knowing the difference is important.

Select the right markets.

Trade only liquid markets with large enough daily or short-term movements to make trading worthwhile. Just because you can now stay up all night to trade a number of popular markets electronically doesn't mean it's a good idea. As trading activity increases, it may become possible to come home from your day job and trade online at night, but most markets remain too thin, can act erratically, and can be very risky outside of regular trading hours.

You also want to avoid markets where much of the price movement takes place as a gap on the open or in only a few trades. As an electronic trader, that means day trading those markets that are active, "behave" well technically, and have enough of a trading range to give you a chance to make money. If the trading range is too small, slippage and commissions are likely to eat up any profits you get. If the range is too wide, the market may be too volatile and the daily risk too large for you to handle. You want a market that moves smoothly but not one that is too thin and too volatile and can run away from you.

Always use stops.

Not everyone views stops as a good thing because they can knock you out of a position just before a move that produces big profits. They also can keep you out of big trouble, however, by getting you out of a position before a profit turns into a loss or before a small loss becomes a big loss. Unless you like playing with fire, use stops to avoid disaster. As an electronic trader, whenever you submit an order or have an order working, you should have another order parked and ready to submit as soon as the initial order is filled. You should know where you will be wrong when you enter your trade.

Cut your losses short.

If there is any rule that is No. 1 in futures trading, this may be it. Because it also is one of the hardest to follow, successful traders harp on it all the time, insisting traders have to learn to like taking losses and to never let their egos tie them to a poor position. Stock traders may be able to hold onto an investment for a long time, but you cannot hold futures hoping they will "come back."

Like any business, risk management is the key to survival in futures trading. If you lose your stake, you cannot trade. Electronic traders typically have some refined entry techniques, but their tactics may not work on the first attempt. If you have developed a trading method that works, you need to get out quickly when the market doesn't respond as you think it should and preserve your capital for several future forays. How you manage a trade after you are in it is much more important than where you enter a position.

Let your profits run, but...

This rule is often cited as a corollary to cutting your losses short, but a number of traders will tell you it's not always the best idea. Profits tend to evaporate when it's "the market's money," and you don't want to have a good trade turn bad just because you are holding out for a profit that might not be realistic. For many traders, it is better to be out too soon than in too long.

For the electronic trader operating in a short-term setting, a profit target may make a lot of sense. It is another form of discipline that may appeal especially to day traders who are not going for home runs but are just trying to produce solid returns every day. If you know your market and what is typical for it and if your technical analysis reveals the likely extent of market moves, you may want to set up a profit-taking stop based on an amount of money or on some technical measurement.

Another situation that calls for taking profits is when the market suddenly moves in your favor and gives you a windfall gain. Don't look a gift horse in the mouth. Take at least some of the profit, or at least tighten your stop to capture most of the unexpected return. You usually won't get that kind of break in short-term trading.

Be patient.

Electronic traders will have lots of opportunities and can't expect to catch them all. After investing in an expensive computer or a high-powered trading system, some traders figure they have to put their new electronic prowess to work immediately to get some return on their investment. They may see trades where there aren't any or may force the action just because they decided to be traders and now they have to trade something. Patience is probably not a strong suit for most short-term traders, but sometimes it pays just to let the market come to you.

Don't let low discount commission rates determine where you trade.

As the cost of trade execution decreases with electronic order matching, lower commission rates have become the centerpiece of competition among firms. If you are an experienced futures trader who only needs trade execution, you may be attracted by the lure of low discount rates. However, if you are a newcomer to futures, you should probably work with a broker who has witnessed the collective mistakes of hundreds of traders over the years and will pass along as much wisdom as you need. Even those who have traded for a while may be better off with this interaction and information-sharing feedback. "I have never met a successful trader who said his ability was determined by commission rates," one brokerage firm official observes.

Prepare yourself for the psychological challenge of trading online.

Trading has always been a psychological battle, but the tone may change a little in an electronic setting. The changes will be especially noticeable for those trying to make the adjustment to a screen from the trading floor, where they could look another trader in the eye and see and hear and feel the mood of the pit. Value is value, whether in the pit or on the screen, but who will be the first to try to find or test that value online? If the floor locals are gone, who will make the bids and who will make the offers? Will screen traders be willing to dangle bids and offers online to see who bites, or will they hang back, waiting for someone else to post their price first?

Electronic trading at home can be a lonely world—no broker, no office chit-chat, no fellow traders to test a market opinion or to commiserate with after a bad trade... You are hanging by the thin thread of an Internet line to a world that wants to wipe out your trading account. When you have a technological glitch, you will feel especially lonely and vulnerable. As long as your connections hold up, you will have more control over your trading, but that means you also are the only one responsible for your trading errors. You probably will make the same mistakes as you did in the past, except electronically, they will happen faster.

CHAPTER 7

The Last Chapter... or the Next Chapter?

*A*s *I was contemplating how to end this book, the doorbell rang. I went downstairs and answered the door. It was UPS delivering my new Globex terminal.*

Well, now I was excited—and a little scared. I had taken all of the classes at the exchange, and all I needed to get off and running was for the telephone company to hook up my new terminal.

Weeks went by, and finally, the phone company finished laying its cable, adding a new modem and phone jacks and hooking up other equipment. It took at least seven hours for the phone people to complete the setup.

At last, it was time to trade online. This was the big night. I turned on my machine, typed in my user ID and my password, and I was ready to trade. This just might be the beginning of the future of futures for me, I thought. But because I am a second-generation floor broker used to yelling and waving my arms around in the open-outcry pits at the Chicago Mercantile Exchange, this new terminal was very threatening.

Getting the courage to go ahead, I set up my page with the markets I wanted to trade. This night, I was looking at the Globex E-mini S&P contract. It gave me the bid and offer of the market. I looked at my research points (support and resistance areas) and decided to buy one E-mini. With one click of my mouse, my order was in and was filled. Wow, was that fast!

The first thing I did was panic. What if the system goes down? How will I get out? Thank goodness, my clearinghouse had given me the phone number of its 24-hour support staff. I felt a lot better knowing I could trade all night if I wanted to, or I could call my order desk to cover my position if I needed to do that.

The first night I traded five contracts a side (five buys / sells). I lost $350. I guess this was tuition for my learning experience.

I went to bed late and had to wake up early, but I couldn't wait to get to work to trade on my computer there. This new machine was very addictive. In the day session, I traded 15 contracts a side. Now I was hooked.

In my first week or two of electronic trading, I lost money. It's not easy doing it this new way, but I know if I educate myself properly, I can learn to trade from home or my office.

It's on to the next chapter.

Although some of the remarks in this book may seem discouraging—even disparaging—about the outlook for electronic trading, it is only because we aren't "there" yet. True electronic futures trading probably won't come as quickly as many would like or as slowly as others would hope, but the trend clearly is in that direction.

Just as the traders of the 1950s and 1960s saw the butter and eggs pits fade away, so will the open-outcry pits of today fade into history unless there is some revolutionary new development in how they operate or someone wants to keep them alive as a backup in case technology fails... as it already has a number of times, giving open-outcry diehards hope that at least some vestige of open-outcry can remain alive a lot longer than most people expect.

The transition to the screen for trading is not an easy one to make for any participant—for the floor trader whose career is changed, for the individual trader who may have to think differently, or for the software developers and system designers who have the challenge of building structures that will hold up in the toughest of market conditions. If not for the fact that electronic trading is faster, more flexible, more efficient, and provides a level playing field for every trader of any size, we might not have to think about moving away from the open-outcry environment.

Online traders tend to be younger, more confident (maybe even a little cocky), more active, and more demanding in their information needs. Those factors probably explain why they are online in the first place. If they wanted to buy only one option, they wouldn't need to be online.

The reality is that as it is in many other areas, technology is the driving force changing how people can trade. Traders already have more data, information, and analytical tools at their finger-tips than the largest institutions just a few years ago. Personal computers date back only to the early 1980s and the Internet only to the mid-1990s, but they have already transformed these areas of trading.

However, one of the Internet sites we checked summarized it best: "The next frontier is really more about communication, not computerization. Connectivity is everything." As an active trader, you must have reliable connections in place, ones that you can count on consistently. To keep things in perspective, fu-tures traders eager to tap the potential of electronic trading need to remember how long it took automobiles, airplanes, electricity, telephones, and television to reach today's levels. They aren't perfect, as satellite failures and power outages have reminded traders in recent years.

Building on that comparison, Bill Massey, an institutional broker at LFG LLC in Chicago, says, "Broker order-entry sys-tems have become relatively stable applications, but they are hooked into rickety stagecoaches (TOPS) riding over rough ter-rain (the floor)—and exchanges don't even know what the ter-rain they are going to is. You can build a Ferrari, but you still have the bad terrain. Exchanges need to build the roads—the telecommunications—to reduce the number of switches, tolls, and stops a trade has to go through. The least friction creates the most trades. What we have today is very sophisticated but rinky-dink at the end."

So what do we think the electronic trader will see in the next few years? Some of the following may fall into the "dream" category or may take longer to develop, but here are some things we envision:

- *Everything will get better technologically.* If the futures industry could just do as well as the securities industry with electronic trading, many traders would be happy. Some facets of electronic futures trading are already working very well, but everything still has to work together consistently to build traders' confidence in the system. In the meantime, remember that the computer and electronic era is still in its infancy, and the futures industry is still in the Pac-man stage. No electronic trader should be without some backup and a support system, including a 24-hour "emergency" phone number at the brokerage firm's order desk.

- *The Internet will continue to grow from being just a telephony network where the computer has simply replaced the phone to transfer files and capture text, graphics, data, etc.* Instead, the current anemic version of the Internet will shift into a global multimedia information-processing utility, according to Art Tursh, senior systems engineer at the CME. This is a global digital convergence phenomena with implications far beyond financial markets and trading, of course, but for traders it means they will have unlimited resources available, including real-time video. In short, while development of the Internet in the last few years may seem amazing, today's version is only a harbinger of what's to come. You ain't seen nothing yet.

- *Access to the Internet will get faster and cheaper and more stable for a much broader audience.* Two-pair telephone wires and 56K modems won't be the answer, but our vision isn't very clear on whether the distribution winner for high-speed connections will be cable, DSL phone service, satellite, wireless, or some new innovation. Cable would seem to have the current numbers edge if it capitalizes on its presence in millions of homes it already has.

- *Trading systems will offer direct market access to anyone with a powerful enough PC.* The trader will have a front-end package that includes real-time quotes, charts, and analysis studies and can do all the order-entry and accounting functions, in other words, all the bells and whistles. The source for all this power may be the broker. When a trader enters an order on this system, a server sorts out which "exchange" gets it, executes the trade, and reports the fill within seconds. The trader will not know—or care, probably—where the trade was made or who made it. Some day, an account statement may look more like a phone bill, with charges for a data feed, news service, broker, clearing organization, and the like, together on one monthly statement.

- *Although egos and political considerations will make it difficult, the futures industry will agree on some more standardized trading platforms into which everyone can plug.* Currently, there is no universal standard among exchanges or among brokers for entering, handling, or executing trades. A one-world, one-system-fits-all solution is not necessary, but there will have to be more of a move to open-architecture system designs that accept a variety of application program interfaces. If a Globex$_3$ is Internet-based, for example, a Globex terminal may become a thing of the past.

- *Common clearing has been and remains a need, including not only futures and options but over-the-counter and other derivative instruments as well.* It should be easier to achieve electronically, if there is a will to make it happen. The clearing organization may not be tied to an exchange, but it could be a separate service bureau, for example, which combines the clearing functions of all U.S. exchanges that are members of the Futures Industry Network.

- *Futures and options and equities may all have the same regulator and may all be traded in the same account.* It may not happen in the next five years, but it should happen eventually. An electronic trader who has a stock portfolio and would like to use futures for short-term protection against a potential market decline must now set up a separate futures account. A person trading E-mini futures who would like to trade S&P 100 Index options (OEX) has to have a separate securities account. And futures traders with smaller accounts find it much more difficult to go short in a securities account.

  Eventually, Congress will bring the Securities and Exchange Commission and the Commodity Futures Trading Commission together as one regulatory agency, and an investment account covering all trading instruments may become possible. That will require a paradigm shift by brokers registered for securities only or brokers registered for futures only, but it would give investors more flexibility. With technology, a combined account should not be an impossible task.

- *Education and training will become more important, from both a trading and a technology standpoint.* It may come from a broker, a trading advisor, a mentor, or some other service, whatever, because people new to trading or new to a software program or making the transition from stocks to futures will need assistance. Opening a trading account does not mean everyone understands what a limit or stop order does or that soybeans are priced in bushels and cocoa in metric tons.

  With all the data and information available on the Internet and the power of today's analytical software programs, customers may think they know all they need to know and don't have to do any work. The challenge for the futures industry will be educating them about how markets and charts and trading systems really operate before they make trades that could wipe out their accounts.

- *A second education challenge will be for brokers and vendors to train their own personnel better.* Many employees do not know or understand what they are selling. They sell what can go right, not what to do when things go wrong. With advances in technology, firms need to be prepared to help customers in that area as well as with trading. (NOTE: We said some items might be dreams.)

- *Discount commission rates will get even lower as technology reduces the cost of order execution and as brokers continue to use rates as their competitive edge.* Online traders will have almost the same leverage as the large institutional traders once had in negotiating lower rates.

- *There will be fewer brokerage firms and traditional exchanges in five years.* By some estimates, mergers and competition could cut the number of futures commission merchants to 25 percent of what there are today. Economic reality has already reduced the number of exchanges or pushed them into alliances. We can't rule out a number of electronic exchanges popping up on the Internet, but time will sort out how many of those survive.

- *Liquidity will be greater, and in some cases much greater, in an electronic setting.* As computers and order-entry systems become more familiar and easier to use, more participants will produce more volume and a more fluid market. Computers may never match the trading floor as a price-discovery mechanism in fast-market conditions, but the challenge for exchanges that supply liquidity today will be to maintain that liquidity and tight bid/ask spreads in the transition period as the market moves from a declining open-outcry forum to an uncertain screen existence.

- *Despite all the hype, trading will not be easier electronically.* If a person thinks electronic trading is the route to utopia and a way to get out of working and doing a real job, she or he is likely to be in for a big surprise. There will be success stories, but will you be one of them? The chance for success in any type of trading often depends on a person's psychological makeup, and that is probably more true in short-term electronic trading than in any other type of trading. Bad habits lead to bad trading; it just happens faster in an electronic environment.

- *On the other hand, the advantage of electronic trading is that you will be able to trade from almost any place at almost any time in almost any market.* With laptops—the "office in a box"—and Palm Pilots and wireless phones and other devices likely to come, technology means a degree of freedom and flexibility never before possible. For many traders, that itself is a great trade, and what makes an electronic future so exciting.

ABOUT THE AUTHORS

Scott Slutsky is a former member of the Chicago Mercantile Exchange's prestigious Board of Directors. Elected in 1989, he is one of the youngest members ever to serve. Slutsky has been a member of the Merc for 22 years and owns and operates Vantage Commodity Corp. and Vantage Learning Center. He is a popular speaker at conferences and seminars around the country. Mr. Slutsky can be reached at **slew1@aol.com,** or visit his Internet site at **www.vantagecorp.com.**

Darrell Jobman is the former editor in chief of *Futures* magazine and has been writing about and editing subjects related to agricultural and financial markets for 30 years. He is the editor of *The Handbook of Technical Analysis*, author of *Bar Chart Basics*, a contributor to *Multiply Your Money: A Beginner's Guide to Commodity Speculation,* and author of numerous articles for publications in the futures industry.

Slutsky and Jobman also worked together to produce *Masters of the Futures*, featuring interviews of 20 prominent leaders in the futures industry and published by McGraw-Hill early in 1999.

INDEX

Aberration (Trade System Inc.), 68
ABG Investment Group, 90
AbleSys Corp. (ASCTrend), 54
About.com Inc., 42
Access-Direct Discount Trading, 90
Account statement page, 82
Account status page, 82
ADM Investor Services, 90
ADSL. *see* Asymmetrical Digital Sub-
   scriber Line (ADSL)
Advantages in Options, 90
AgriWeather, 39
AIQ Systems (TradingExpert Pro), 55
Alaron Trading Corp., 90–92, 91 *il.*
Allendale Inc., 92
Alpha One Trading (A1T), 92
Altavest Worldwide Trading Inc., 92–93
American Futures & Options, 93
Analysis tools, 14
Angus Jackson, 93
Application program interfaces (APIs),
   139
ARC Systems Inc., 55
Arrow Futures & Options, 93
ASCTrend (AbleSys Corp.), 54
Aspen Graphics, 55
Asymmetrical Digital Subscriber Line
   (ADSL), 11–12
A1T (Alpha One Trading), 92
Auditrack, 93
Avid Traders Chat, 47

Babson, Roger, 64
Beddows Commodities Inc., 94
Behold! (Investors Technical Services), 59
BEST Direct. *See* Peregrine Financial
   Group
Best Direct, 119–120, 119 *il.*
Bloomberg, 17
Breakouts, 166–167
   trading opening range, 167–168
Bressert, Walter, 55
Bridge, 18
Bridge/CRB MarketCenter Plus, 18
Brite Futures Inc., 31
Brokerage firms, 14. *see also* Online
   brokerage firms
Brokers, discount, 71–72
BrokerTec, 140
Brower, William, 36
Buffalo Trading Group Inc., 94

Bulletin board services, 46–48
Bullish Review, 37
Bureau of Economic Analysis, 45–46
Buy stop, 159

Cable service, 12
Cablesoft Inc. (LiveWire), 56
Call markets, 139
Cancel/cancel-replace page, 81
CA-NI Industries Ltd. (Wisdom of the
   Ages), 55
Cannon Trading Co. Inc., 94
Cantor Exchange, 140–141, 148
Capital Management Sciences (InSite), 26
Capitol Commodity Services Inc., 94
CBOE. *see* Chicago Board Options
   Exchange (CBOE)
CBOT. *see* Chicago Board of Trade
   (CBOT)
Channels
   breakouts, 166–167
   trading within, 166
Chat rooms, 46–48
Chicago Board of Trade (CBOT), 133,
   144–148
Chicago Board Options Exchange
   (CBOE), 134
Chicago Futures, 94
Chicago Futures Investment Group
   (Futureswatch), 95
Chicago Mercantile Exchange (CME), 15,
   134, 138, 142–144
Chicago Tribune, 35
Choice Daytrades, 56
Cisco Futures, 31
Citynet PLC, 26
Clayburg Custom Programming (Cyclone
   System), 56
Clearing organizations, 189
Cleartrade Commodities, 95
Clearwater Commodities, 95
Club 3000, 37
CME. *see* Chicago Mercantile Exchange
   (CME)
CME Universal Broker Station (CUBS),
   77, 135–137
Coast Investment Software Inc., 56
Collective, The (International Trading
   Systems), 59
Columbia Asset Management, 95
COMMODEX, 56

Commodit-e-zine, 36
Commodity Café, 47
Commodity Central, 41
Commodity Floor Brokers and Traders
    Association (CFBTA), 44
Commodity Futures and Options Service,
    95
Commodity Futures Trading Commission
    (CFTC), 45
Commodity Systems Inc. (CSI), 31
Commodity Timing, 40
Commoditytrade.net, 22
Commodity Traders Club News, 37
Commodity Trend Service, 22
Compas Financial, 96
Computers, for pretrade analysis, 8–9
Computrade (Futures Conferences Ltd.),
    58
Confirmation page, 80
ConNETics Technology Group, 56
CQG, 18–19
Creative Breakthrough Inc., 57
Crown Futures Corp., 96
CTS Financial Publishing Inc., 22
CUBS. see CME Universal Broker Station
    (CUBS)
Currency Management Corp., 96–97
CyBerCorp.com, 97
Cyclone System (Clayburg Custom
    Programming), 56

Dallas Commodity Co. Inc., 97
Data Broadcasting Corp. (DBC), 26
Data Transmission Network Corp. (DTN),
    19
Datek, 139
Day orders, 161
DayTrader Corporation, 40
Day trading, 161–164
Dedicated telephone lines, 10–11
DH Financial LLC, 98
Dinapoli, Joe, 56
Discount brokers, 71–72
Discount commission rates, 183, 190
Discount Futures Brokerage, 98
Distribution systems, 9–13
    ADSL, 11–12
    cable service, 12
    dedicated telephone lines, 10–11
    fixed wireless, 13
    ISDN, 11–12
    satellite dish, 12–13

Dow Jones Company, 34–35
Dr. Ed Yardeni's Economics Network, 24
Drummond Geometry (THA Inc.), 66
DSL. see Asymmetrical Digital Subscriber
    Line (ADSL)
Dynacomp Inc., 57
DynaStore, 57

E. D. & F. Man International Inc., 77,
    114–115
ECommodities, 98
efutures.com, 100
Ehrlich Commodity Futures, 57
Eiger Group, The, 100
Electronic analysis. see Pretrade analysis
Electronic Communications Networks
    (ECNs), 139–141
Electronic futures traders
    backups for, 187–188
    controlling technology and, 178
    cutting losses short and, 182
    discipline and, 180
    discount commission rates and, 183
    education and training for, 190
    future, 187–191
    impulsive behavior and, 178–179
    market knowledge and, 181
    market selection and, 181
    patience and, 183
    requirements for becoming, 4
    stops and, 181–182
Electronic futures trading
    defined, 3–4
    difficulty of, 155
    plans for, 179–180
    psychology of, 183–184
    rules for, 177–184
    standardized platforms for, 189
Electronic futures trading approaches,
    161–164
    flexible, 171–175
    reactions to events or reports, 170–171
    trade support/resistance, 169–170
    trading opening range breakout,
        167–168
    trading within channel breakout,
        166–167
    trading within trending channel,
        165–166
E-mini S&P, 142–143
E-mini stock index contracts, 174–175

End-of-day, historical data, 31–33
Ensign Software, 57
Entrypoint 2000i (Software Solutions), 65
Equis International Inc. (MetaStock), 57
eSignal, 26, 27 *il.*
Essex Trading Co. Ltd., 58
Eurex, 133, 138, 144–145, 148–149
Excel Futures, 100
Excel Systems, 100
Excel Trading Group, 101
Exchanges
    Cantor Exchange, 140–141, 148
    Chicago Board of Trade, 133, 144–148
    Chicago Mercantile Exchange, 134,
        142–144
    Eurex, 133, 138, 144–145, 148–149
    history of, 133–134
    London International Financial
        Futures and Optioons Exchange,
        149–150
    New York Mercantile Exchange, 138,
        148
    Sydney Futures Exchange, 151
    trading systems of, 134–142
    Web sites for, 151–154
EXPO (Leading Market Technologies), 60

FACS Journalists' Guide to Economic
    Terms, 43
Far Financial Inc., 101
Farm Bureau/ACRES, 28
Fast market, 161
FCMs. *see* Futures commission merchants
    (FCMs)
Field Financial Group, 101
Fill or kill (FOK) order, 160
Fill report, 81–82
Financial Facilitators, 58
Financial information Management Inc.
    (ProphetX), 19
First American Discount Corp., 101–102
First Internet National Directory (FIND),
    41
Fixed wireless, 13
Flexible trading approaches, 171–175
Floor traders, 71
FM signals, 13
FOK (fill or kill) order, 160
Fontanills, George, 63
Forums, 46–48
Fox Investments, 102

Freeman & Co., 102
Futech Commodity Services, 102–103
FutureLink NS, 28
Futurelink Pro, 19–20
FuturesBusiness, 104
Futures commission merchants (FCMs),
    134
Futures Conferences Ltd. (Computrade),
    58
Futures Direct, 103
Futures Discount Group, 103
Futures Industry Association (FIA), 43
Futures Industry (magazine), 36
Futures Magazine, 35–36
Futures.Net, 22
FuturesOnline, 103, 104 *il.*
FutureSource/Bridge LLC, f20
Futures traders. *see* Electronic futures
    traders
Futures trading. *see also* Electronic
    futures trading
        history of, 133–134
        order processing systems for, 134–142
Futures Truth Co., 38
Futureswatch (Chicago Futures Invest-
    ment Group), 95
Futuresweb.com, 23
FutureWise Trading Group, 105

Genesis Financial Data Services, 31–32
Glance Market Data Services, 32
Global Forex Trading Ltd., 105
Global Trade Execution (GTEX), 98, 99 *il.*
GlobalView Software Inc., 58
Globex, 137–138, 142–144, 145 *il.*, 189
Good 'til canceled (GTC) orders, 161

Hall, Alan, 64
Historical data, end-of-day, 31–33
Hi-Tech Futures Inc., 105
HyperFeed Technologies Inc., 28

Impulsive behavior, electronic traders
    and, 178
Infinity Brokerage Services, 105–106
InSite (Capital Management Sciences), 26
Instinet, 139
Institute for Options Research (Option
    Master), 58
Institute of Finance and Banking at the
    University of Göttingen, 41

Institutional Advisory Services Group
   (IASG), 42
Integrated Services Digital Network
   (ISDN), 11–12
Interactive Brokers LLC, 106, 107
International Federation of Technical
   Analysts, 43
International Futures Exchange Ltd., 137
International Trading Systems (The
   Collective), 59
Internet, 187, 188
   online order entry and, 76–78
Interquote, 28
Intersat Space Communications Corp., 39
Interval-based trading, 94
Introducing Brokers (IBs), 77–78
Investing, essentials for, 1
Investment Engineering Corp., 59
Investment Reference, 42
InvestorLinks.com, 23
Investor/RT (Linn Software Inc.), 60
Investorsoftware.com, 59
Investors Technical Services (Behold!), 59
Iowa Electronic Market, 141
Iowa Grain Co., 106–108
Ira Epstein & Co. Futures, 77, 108, 109 *il.*
IRIS, 59–60
ISDN. *see* Integrated Services Digital
   Network (ISDN)

Jack Carl Futures, 108–110, 111 *il.*
Joe Krutsinger Inc., 60
Jones Ag Marketing, 110
Jones Financial Network (PC Trader), 29

Kaiser, Bill, 75
Kase & Co. Inc., 60
Kelly, Roy, 55
Keystone Discount Commodity Brokers,
   110

Lakefront Futures & Options LLC, 110
Leading Market Technologies (EXPO), 60
LFG LLC (Linnco Futures Group), 114
LIFFE CONNECT, 150
LIFFE (London International Financial
   Futures and Options Exchange),
   149–150
Limit order, 158
Lind, Barry, 112
Lind-Waldock & Co., 112, 113 *il.*

Link Futures, 112–113
Linnco Futures Group (LFG LLC), 114
Linn Software Inc. (Investor/RT), 60
Liquid markets, 181, 191
Listen Only Squawk Box, 39
LiveWire (Cablesoft Inc.), 56
Logical Information Machines Inc., 32
London International Financial Futures
   and Options Exchange (LIFFE),
   149–150

M. Gordon Publishing Group, 37
McKnight, Paul, 94
Main entry order page, for online order
   entry systems, 78–80
Marketforum.com, 47
Market if touched (MIT) order, 158
Market on close (MOC) order, 160
Market on opening (MOO) order, 160
Market orders, 157–158
Market Research Inc., 29
Market Technicians Association, 44
Massey, Bill, 187
MATIF, 138
Matrix Trading Group Inc., 115
Mentality, for trading, 2–3
Meppen Trading LLC, 115
Merchant Capital Inc., 115
MetaStock (Equis International Inc.),
   57–58
MG Financial Group, 116
MicroStar Research and Trading Inc., 62
Mindfire Systems, 62
MIT (market if touched) order, 158
Mobeo Inc., 29
MOC (market on close) order, 160
Money, investing and, 1–2
MOO (market on opening) order, 160

National Agricultural Statistics Service
   (NASS), 46
National Futures Association (NFA), 45
National Trading Group Inc., 62
Net Discount Futures, 116
NetFutures, 116
NetTraderRT, 62
NeuroShell Trader (Ward Systems
   Group), 69
Newsgroups, 46–48
News Sources, 33–34
New York Mercantile Exchange, 138, 148

New York Times, The, 35
New Zealand Futures Exchange, 137
NextTrend Analytical Services Inc., 20
Nihon Unicom Corp., 117
Nirvana Systems Inc. (Omni Trader), 62
Non-U.S. exchanges, 16 *il.*
North American Quotations Inc., 29
NPA Futures Inc., 63

OCO (one cancels the other) order, 161
Office for Futures and Options Research,
   The, 44
Omega Research Inc., 48, 53–54
Omni Trader (Nirvana Systems Inc.), 62
One cancels the other (OCO) order, 161
Online brokerage firms. *see also* Online
   order entry systems; individual
   brokerage firm
   checklist for, 87–88 *il.*
   evaluating, 85–89
   key questions for, 83–85
Online order entry, 156–167
   correct, 156
   Internet and, 76–78
Online order entry systems, 72–75. *see
   also* Online brokerage firms
   computer screens for, 78–83
      account statement page, 82
      account status page, 82
      cancel/cancel-replace page, 81
      confirmation page, 80
      fill report, 81–82
      main entry order page, 78–80
      preview order page, 80
      quote pages, 82–83
   Internet and, 76–78
   mistakes and, 75–76
Online order processing systems
   CME Universal Broker Station
      (CUBS), 135–137
   Globex, 137–138
   Project A, 137–138
   Trade Order Processing System
      (TOPS), 134–135
Oops tactic, 168
Opening range breakouts, 167–168
Open orders, 161
Open-outcry trading system, 138
Option Dynamics, 63
Optionetics, 63

Option Master (Institute for Options
   Research), 58
Optionomics Corp. (Orion Risk Manage-
   ment System), 63
OptionsAnalysis.com, 63
OptionVue Systems International Inc., 64
Option Wizard Online, 63
Op Wiz Inc., 117
Or better, 158
Order entry, 156–157. *see also* Online
   order entry
   correct, 156
   Internet and, 76–78
Order-entry mechanisms, 14
Orion Futures Group Inc., 117
Orion Risk Management System
   (Optionomics Corp.), 63
Orphelin, Pierre, 65

Paragon Investments Inc., 117
PAT Systems Ltd., 118
Peacock Trading Inc., 118
Pearce Financial, 118–119
Peregrine Financial Group Inc. (PFG),
   119–120
PFG (Peregrine Financial Group),
   119–120
Pinnacle Data, 32
Pinson Communications, 38
PMB (Professional Market Brokerage),
   121
Portals, 21–24
Pretrade analysis, 7–8
   data and information sources for,
      13–17
   distribution systems for, 9–13
   hardware for, 8–13
   software for, 48–52
Preview order page, for online order entry
   systems, 80
Pricecharts.com, 32
Price Futures Group Inc., 120
Price history, 15
Price quotes, 14, 15, 24–25
Prime Time Investment Services Inc., 121
Professional Market Brokerage (PMB),
   121
Profits, 182–183
Profitunity Trading Group, 64
Project A, 137–138, 145–148, 147 *il.*
Promised Land Technologies Inc., 64

Prophet Financial Systems, 33
Publication sources, 33–35. *see also*
  specific source

Quant Trading Inc., 121
Quote.com, 30
Quote pages, 82–83
Quotes. *see* Price quotes
Quote services, 25

R. J. O'Brien & Associates Inc., 123
Rand Financial Services Inc., 121–122
Raschke, Linda, 40
Real-time data, 26–30
Real-time quotes, 15–16
Real Traders, 48
Reeder, Chuck, 2
Refco Group Ltd., 122–123
Reinhard Investment Management, 64
Resistance, trade, 169–170
Reuters News Service, 21, 34–35
Rina Systems, 64
Risk management, 182
Robbins Trading Co., 123
Rosenthal Collins Group LLC, 124
R.S. & Associates, 124–125
Ruggiero, Murray, 65
Ruggiero Associates, 65

Saddle River Futures Trading Group Inc.,
  125
SAFIR-X (SirTrade International), 65
Satellite dishes, 12–13
Scale trading, 94
Securities and Exchange Commission
  (SEC), 45
Sell order, 159
Silicon Investor, 48
SirTrade International (SAFIR-X), 65
Site-by-Site!, 23–24
SMART Futures, 125
SMOTASS, 41
Soft Trade Inc., 47
Software Solutions (Entrypoint 2000i), 65
Spectrum Commodities, 125
S&P 500 Index E-mini contract, 142
Spread order, 159
S&P Scalper Software, 65
Stahr, Dennis, 42
Standard & Poor's Comstock, 30
STA Trading Services, 126

Stoll Momentum System Inc., 65
Stop close only order, 160
Stop limit order, 160
Stop order, 158–159
  buy, 159
  sell, 159
Stops, 181–182
Striker Securities Inc., 126
Stuckey, Randy, 62
Sunny Harris & Associates Inc., 40
Super Fund Financial Group Inc., 126
Support, trade, 169–170
Sydney Futures Exchange, 151

TechHackers, 66
Technical Analysis of Stocks & Commodi-
  ties, 36
Technical Tools, 33
Technology, 166–167
Technology, controlling, and electronic
  traders, 178
Telephone service, dedicated, 10–11
TFC Commodity Charts, 24
THA Inc. (Drummond Geometry), 66
Tick Data Inc., 33
Tierra del Fuego Ltd., 66
Titan Trading Analytics (Virtual Trader),
  66
Tom Jackson's DayTrader, 40
Top Gun Trading Systems Inc., 66
TOPS. *see* Trade Order Processing
  System (TOPS)
Track Data Corp., 30
Trade Center Inc., 126–128, 127 *il.*
Tradehard.com, 24
Trade Order Processing System (TOPS),
  76–77, 134–135
Trade reactions, 170–171
Trade resistance, 169–170
Traders. *see* Electronic futures traders
Traders Auction, 42
Trader's Edge, 66
Traders Library, 38
Trader's Network Inc., 128
Traders Press Inc., 38
Traders Software Co. Inc. (TSCI), 67
Trader's Toolbox, 67
TraderWare X, 67
TradeSignals.com, 67
TradeStorm Inc., 67
Trade support, 169–170

Trade System Inc. (Aberration), 68
Trade with the trend rule, 164–166
TradingExpert Pro (AIQ Systems), 55
Trading mentality, 2–3
Trading platform services, 16–17
Trading process, 5 *il.*
Trading systems
    open-outcry, 138
    software for, 48–52
Trading Systems International Inc., 68
Trading Techniques Inc. (Advanced GET),
    68
Trading Technologies, 68
Trading within channels, 166
Trending channel, 165–167
Trend Reflection Trading System, 68
Trendsetter Software, 68
Trester, Ken, 58
Trident Trading Systems Ltd., 69
TSCI (Traders Software Co. Inc.), 67
TS Express, 36
Tursh, Art, 188

Ultra Trading Analytics Inc., 69
U.S. Department of Agriculture (USDA),
    46
U.S. Federal Reserve Board, 45
U.S. futures exchanges, monthly fees, 16
    il.
U.S. stock exchanges, monthly fees, 16 *il.*

VALUES API (Virtual Access Link Using
    Exchange Services—Application
    Programming Interface), 149
VIP Futures, 128–129
Virtual Trader (Titan Trading Analytics),
    66
Vision LP, 129

Waldemar's List, 41
Walter Bressert Futures Online, 55
Ward Systems Group (NeuroShell
    Trader), 69
Web sites, for futures traders, 21–24. *see
    also* specific Web site
Williams, Larry, 168
Window on Wallstreet Inc., 21
Wisdom of the Ages (CA-NI Industries
    Ltd.), 55
Working orders page, 80
World Link Futures Inc., 129
World Wide Web. *see* Internet

Xpresstrade LLC, 130

ZAP Futures, 130–132, 131 *il.*
ZDNet Anchor Desk, 38